Praise for *Active Dreaming*

"*Active Dreaming* is a soul-nurturing, imagination-firing book! Avowed storyteller and webmaster of dream landscapes Robert Moss challenges us to dream *forward* into our personal and collective futures to give the Great Story of humanity meaning and purpose. The dreamscapes he conjures are full of surprises and hope!"

— Dorothea Hover-Kramer, psychotherapist and author of *Second Chance at Your Dream* and *Healing Touch*

"If you are searching for a way to reconnect with your authentic self, read *Active Dreaming* by Robert Moss. This book's timeless techniques and thoughtful guidance will bring you back to the springs of personal wholeness. I highly recommend it."

— Robert Waggoner, author of *Lucid Dreaming*

"Robert Moss's *Active Dreaming* prescribes medicine to heal the pervasive drought of dreams in our society. From stories to dreams to instructions on how to navigate the bountiful ocean of dreaming, we readers journey toward the heart of what it is to be human. Illuminating, compassionate, and practical, *Active Dreaming* will inspire dreamers of all ages and walks of life everywhere."

— Denyse Beaudet, PhD, author of *Dreamguider: Open the Door to Your Child's Dreams*

"Dreaming may be our most important natural resource, one that everyone has access to and one that can never run out. Robert Moss teaches us how to tap that resource for the benefit of our waking lives and the healing of our world. Robert is a wizard of the Dreamways and a master teacher. In this exciting, outstanding book he works his special magic, giving us practical tools for bringing our dreams to life and our lives to dream. No one does it better."

— David Spangler, author of *Subtle Worlds: An Explorer's Field Notes*

"Robert Moss's invitation to 'wake up and dream' opens the door to the world within the world of our sleeping and waking dream life, where the self merges with the Self. In a book both enchanting and practical, he provides the compass and map for the journey and serves as wise, compassionate, and soulful guide."

— Judy Reeves, author of *A Writer's Book of Days*

"Robert Moss's extraordinary dreamwork, in my opinion, comes from the fact that he is not confined, as are we psychologists, to scientific rationale, methods, and explanations. Instead, his background in journalism has opened his mind as a storyteller. In *Active Dreaming*, Moss helps us explore the immense possibilities in consciousness that our dreams reveal, leaving us in a new world of meaning and adventure."

— Henry Reed, PhD, author of *Dream Medicine*,
known as the father of the modern dreamwork movement

"This book sits at the intersection of poetry and practicality. Robert Moss speaks to a world we each inhabit and only dimly understand. Read this book. You will be a little more awake and a little clearer, and you will probably greet the world with a little more acceptance."

— Peter Block, coauthor of *The Abundant Community*

"*Active Dreaming* is a jewel of a book! This is an important, practical guide providing powerful tools to chart a way to choose and live the life we desire. Robert Moss's teachings are clear and empowering. *Active Dreaming* is a book that we can continue to turn to for deep wisdom, rich teachings, and inspiration time and time again. This book not only helps us to personally transform our lives but also provides a path to transform the world we live in."

— Sandra Ingerman, MA, author of
Soul Retrieval and *How to Thrive in Changing Times*

"In *Active Dreaming*, Robert Moss shows how we can be active participants in our dream world. *Active Dreaming* is one of the most practical guidebooks on dreams currently available. Highly recommended."

— Larry Dossey, MD, author of
The Power of Premonitions and *Healing Words*

ACTIVE DREAMING

To the midwives
of a dreaming society

Contents

Part Three. Toward a Commonwealth of Dreamers

PROLOGUE

Making Every Day a Holiday

Today is the first day of your new life. When you opened this book, you put yourself on a road that will lead you to manifest your life dreams. To follow this road, you'll want to define who you are and what your life project is all about. This is essential, because the human being is an animal that must define itself or else be defined by others. Let others tell you who you are, and you can find yourself trapped in the cage of other people's needs and expectations rather quickly. You can find yourself stuck inside a frame and required to forever remain the same. You might be bent double under the weight of a past history you want to let go of but can't because others keep strapping it on your back. You might find it hard to breathe under the low ceilings of the little box houses of other people's limiting beliefs about the world and your role in it.

This book will help you get out of those cages and frames and chart your own course in life, to a place of wild creative freedom I call the Place of the Lion. To get there, you need to find your essential life story and tell it and live it so that others can receive it. If you don't know that your life has an essential story, then you have probably been trapped in a little story, one of those confining stories spun by others that crush your ribs and pinch your throat so you can't breathe, let alone speak up. You have come to this book because you are ready to break out and claim your bigger story, and to learn to tell it so well that others will not only hear you but also welcome what is most alive and creative in you. When the lion speaks, *everyone* listens.

You are going to learn an approach to life that I call Active Dreaming. This approach includes paying attention to night dreams, but it is not only, or even essentially, about what happens at night. It is a method for conscious living. When you become an active dreamer, you'll notice that the world speaks to you in a different way.

As I write these lines, I am poked by a friend on Facebook with a quote from Henry David Thoreau: "Go confidently in the direction of your dreams. Live the life you have imagined."

This quote is hardly obscure; there's a whole industry devoted to re-producing it on T-shirts, aprons, posters, bangles, and fridge magnets. Maybe you have it on a coffee mug, as I do.

Thoreau's words are brilliant, practical advice for conscious living, but only if we can brush off the cliché dust that settles when something is quoted so often that it loses its punch.

So try this, right *now*, with the words in front of you. Say them out loud. Now make them your own by saying something like: "I go confidently in the direction of my dreams. I am living the life I've imagined."

Are you feeling some forward movement? It requires a next step. You now want to decide on one thing you'll do today (or tonight) to act on what is now your living, personal affirmation that you are following your dreams (present tense) and you are living the life you've imagined. Don't be vague, and for goodness' sake don't try to be spiritually correct. You'll do one thing to get a great life plan working. Could be as simple as filling that Thoreau mug with another jolt of java to make sure you're wired for some fabulous problem-solving or creative effort — or some chamomile tea to make you sweet and mellow.

This little plan for brushing the cliché dust off Thoreau is an example of the practice of Active Dreaming as a way of conscious living. We receive what the world gives us as a prompt to turn in a certain direction and make a creative choice.

Active dreamers are choosers. We learn to recognize that, whatever situation we are in, we always have a choice. We choose to stop running away from the monster in our dreams — who may turn out to be our own power hunting us — when we brave up and turn around to confront it. We choose not to buy into self-limiting beliefs or the limited models of reality suggested by others. We learn from Viktor Frankl, an exemplary active dreamer, that we can grow a dream of possibility even inside a Nazi death camp — and that when we can grow that dream strong enough it takes us beyond terror and despair to a place of freedom and delight.

In Persian tradition, there is a knightly order of spiritual warriors known as the Fravartis. They choose to enter this world to fight the good fight. They move in this world with the knowledge of a higher world. They are attuned to a secret order of events beyond the facts recorded in the media and our day planners.

Active dreamers engage with this world in a similar way. We are choosers. We know who we are, where we come from, and that our lives have meaning and purpose. And that part of this purpose is to generate meaning and help others to find meaning in their lives at every opportunity. As Viktor Frankl taught us, rising from the hell of Auschwitz, humans require meaning just as they require air and food and water.

Stories are better teachers than theories. This book will help you find your bigger and braver story — the one that can give you the heart and guts to get through the darkest day — and have that story heard and received by others. So let's start with a story from the road, to give you a sense of what it means to be an active dreamer on an ordinary day.

MY FIRST FLIGHT OF THE DAY IS DELAYED, and when we land at Chicago's O'Hare airport a voice mail from the airline informs me that I have missed my connection and have been rebooked, on a combination of flights that will get me to my destination seven hours late, much too late for the dinner and evening event I have planned. Oh joy. But wait —

my watch tells me I may just have time to dash from one end of the vast airport complex to the other and make my connection after all.

When I arrive, breathless, at the departure gate, the plane is still on the ground but the doors were closed one minute ago, and no, there's no way they'll open them. "But you might be able to catch our other flight to Seattle," the gate agent tells me. "It's leaving in thirty minutes." How can this be? The other flight has been delayed more than three hours. Another run, to the other end of the C concourse, where things don't look promising. Above the press of anxious, long-delayed faces, I see on the announcements screen that a dozen people are on standby.

I size up the three gate agents at the desk. One has dressed with slightly more sartorial flair than the others and has a rather exotic name: Valerio. I pick him as the man to consult.

"Valerio," I tell him, "I suspect that you are a magician. And that it will be your pleasure to magic up a seat for me that doesn't currently exist on this flight." He receives this statement matter-of-factly, with just the slightest twitch of the laugh lines around his eyes and mouth. It doesn't look good, he regrets to inform me. I now pull rank, just a little, by mentioning that I fly a lot and therefore have priority status. Okay, that could help, but he can't promise anything. I'll need to check back later.

Twenty minutes later, everyone has boarded the plane except for the standby passengers, who now include me. They are closing the door when suddenly I am slipped a boarding pass, the one that shouldn't exist. Soon I am in a middle seat at the back of the bus, my knees jammed uncomfortably against the back of the seat in front of me. And I'm feeling celebratory.

Maybe picking up on my mood, the fellow sitting to my left initiates a conversation. Soon he's telling me his life story. Stan is a salt-of-the earth, blue-collar guy. He's worked for thirty-three years for the same company, making and marketing fire prevention equipment, and they have treated him well and he feels confident that his pension will be there when he retires. It's the thought of retirement that scares him. Three of his male friends dropped dead within six months of retirement.

He'd like some help with this, and asks me, quite directly, what I would suggest.

"Tell me what you love to do," I respond. "Tell me what you like to do for the sheer pleasure of doing it."

He thinks about this for a bit. Then he says, "I love the water. I used to go scuba diving. I grew up near the water, on Rhode Island, where there's a beach down the block whichever direction you take."

"Are those the beaches you think of when you picture yourself at the water?"

He tells me he's relocated to North Carolina because of his job, and there's a beach he likes there as well.

What else does he like?

"I like being with family, with community." He grew up in a big family, one of twelve siblings. They didn't have much, but they had each other. "And I like giving back." He explains that he and some of his brothers banded together recently to buy their parents a house. As I said, this guy is salt of the earth.

What else does he like? "I like the perfect martini," he says with a naughty grin. "None of them sissy fruit drinks."

I turn the discussion to skills. What is he really good at?

"Cooking breakfast."

I'm surprised by his immediate, unconsidered reply. He recalls that as a kid he was often the one who took charge of getting breakfast on the table for his enormous family. "And I loved doing it. I liked the sense of looking after everybody. And I didn't have to wash the dishes after cooking the bacon."

What else is he good at? He knows a lot about preventing, containing, and putting out fires. He's great in the water and behind a wheel on the road. He's a team player and a connector.

After a while, I say, "I'm going to say a few things to you, and I want you to pretend you are listening to a description of a man you don't know. Would that be okay?"

He's intrigued. I start telling him a story about the passions and skills of a certain man, and his need to bring the two together. As I talk, I raise and lower my cupped hands, as if I'm juggling. As I raise my left hand, closer to the heart, I talk of passions, ranging from giving back and looking after a big family to drinking the perfect martini. As I raise my right hand, I talk of skills, from putting out fires to cooking breakfast.

"So what can you see that guy, who has this combination of passions and skills, doing in the second half of his life?"

Stan thinks for a moment, then says, "Owning and running a diner on the beach in North Carolina."

"A diner. Really?"

"Yes, an old-fashioned family diner."

"Where you cook three hundred breakfasts."

"At least. And where they can mix up one mean martini." There's that naughty grin. "Hey," Stan says, clapping me on the shoulder, "I gotta thank you. I'm feeling more juiced and mobilized than I've felt since I started dating. I'm already working out a business plan for the diner in my head, and I think I know the perfect location for it. I guess you're in the wrong seat on the wrong plane all for me."

He takes a pull on his beer and asks, "What are you going to do when you retire, Robert?"

"You know the answer."

I wait for him to find it. "Oh — right — you're never going to retire, because you love what you do."

"That's right. I think the great trick in life, wherever you are in the journey, is to do what you love and let the universe support it. When we do what we love, every day is a holiday."

I was happy I was in the wrong seat on the wrong plane that day. The wrong plane got me to Seattle airport at the time the right plane was supposed to arrive, though my bag took another twelve hours to catch up with me.

I'll put up with just about anything that has story value, and there was a great story here, one that I retold with gusto at dinner with my students at a training for teachers of Active Dreaming that night.

The story of the man whose dream turned out to be a diner by the beach is a taste of what you are going to find in this book. We do better when we are willing to meet the unexpected and improvise when our plans are screwed up. We do better still when we wake up to the fact that we go through life as synchronicity magnets, attracting to ourselves people and events according to the attitudes and energy we are carrying. When we are charged with purpose, our magnetism increases. When we are following our calling, we move in a natural field of dreams. We draw new allies, events, and resources to us. Chance encounters and benign coincidences support us and ease our passage in ways that are inexplicable to those from whom the spiritual laws of human existence are hidden.

What Stan and I did together on the plane is an everyday example of how we can help each other to grow dreams for life. At the end of that flight, he had his retirement plan, and I had the pleasure of helping him create it. Cooking breakfast for three hundred people in a diner might not be my dream for later life, or yours, but we must never judge how other people follow their chosen callings (as long as they do no harm to others or the earth). The trick is to do what you love and let the world support it. Active dreamers seek to turn all work into play, so that every day is a holiday.

INTRODUCTION

Three Modes of Active Dreaming

Here's an open secret: dreaming is not fundamentally about what happens during sleep. It's about waking up. In ordinary life, we are often in the circumstances of sleepwalkers, going through the motions, trying to keep up with preset schedules and to meet other people's expectations and requirements. We let other people determine what's important. We let them define who we are and what we are able and *not* able to do and become. Ruled by habit and the need to get through the daily grind, we forget that our lives may have a larger purpose.

Dreaming, we wake up to a bigger story. The moment of awakening may come in a sleep dream, when we get out of our own way and it is easier for us to encounter something beyond the projections of the trivial daily mind and the consensual hallucinations that weave much of our default reality. The awakening may come in the liminal zone between sleep and waking that the French used to call *dorveille*, which literally means "sleep-wake." It may come in a flash of illumination during a walk in nature, perhaps at the moment when the sun rises above the mountains and opens a path across a lake. The awakening may be hard won. It may come at the price of illness, defeat, or despair, of events or recurring disappointments that push us down and back so hard we have to re-vision and revalue everything we once held to be given. We may have to go through a dark night of the soul before the sun shines at midnight, as ancient initiates described the moment of entry into the full experience of the Greater Mysteries.

The initiation may come in the way familiar to true shamans, when a power of the deeper life seizes us and tears us apart and consents, when we are re-membered, to become our life ally. Angels can appear as fierce as tigers, or as tigers. We don't really need to hunt our power; our power is forever hunting us. To awaken to the guide in our lives, the one who does not judge us and is with us always, we don't have to cross the desert and fast on the mountaintop, unless we have forgotten that the soul of the soul is always near, and is lost to us only when we are lost to it.

So what is *Active* Dreaming? The phrase is a provocation designed to shake us free from the cozy and constricting assumption that dreaming is a passive activity, something that happens when we go to sleep and that may or may not amount to anything more than random chemical washes in the brain or the processing and dumping of "day residue." I am tremendously grateful for the gift of spontaneous sleep dreams, the ones we don't ask for and often don't want. They hold up a magic mirror in which we can see ourselves as we truly are, which can be embarrassing and mobilizing. They goad us to perform course corrections when we have gone badly off track. They serve as a voice of conscience. They preview challenges and opportunities that lie in our future, giving us the chance to make better choices on our life roads. Sleep dreams show us what is going on inside the body, diagnose developing complaints before medical symptoms present themselves, and show us what the body needs in order to stay well. We solve problems in our sleep and can wake with clarity, energy, and direction in a life project that we lacked the night before. And, as the First Peoples of my native Australia teach, our personal dreams may be a passport to the Dreamtime, which is far more than the Dumpster of the personal subconscious; it is the larger reality in which we can meet the ancestors and our authentic spiritual teachers.

It is the "all-at-once," where the time is always Now, from which the events and situations of our physical lives emanate into the smaller world of clock time and linear sequence.

We say, "I had a dream," not knowing a better way to speak. In truth, it would sometimes be more accurate to say, "A dream had me," because certain dreams do come upon us, as the hawk comes upon the rabbit, talons outstretched. We receive visitations from a friend or family member who has died and who may come with an urgent need or message. We are overwhelmed by a great wave that may be a preview of a tsunami out there in a far ocean, or that may represent the immensity of the power of an emotion rising within us — and perhaps within our family or relationship — that could overwhelm our ordinary reason and balance.

I work with sleep dreams in all these varieties, and many more, and welcome them to work on me. But Active Dreaming is far more than a method for decoding sleep dreams. If you are new to this approach, let me invite you to set aside any prior conceptions of what dream analysis or dream interpretation is here and now, at the door. We are going on a journey to far more exciting places. While the techniques involved are fresh and original, they are also incalculably ancient. We are going to reclaim ways of seeing and knowing and healing that were known to our early ancestors and that kept them alive on a dangerous planet and enabled them to communicate with one another and with other forms of life in the speaking land around them.

Active Dreaming is a way of being fully of this world while maintaining constant contact with another world, the world-behind-the-world, where the deeper logic and purpose of our lives are to be found. It is a way of remembering and embodying what the soul knows about essential things: who we are, where we come from, and what our sacred purpose is in this life and beyond this life. When we lose the knowledge of these essential things, we are lost to our bigger story. Not knowing who we are or what we are meant to become, we can do unthinking harm to ourselves and others.

Active Dreaming is a discipline, as is yoga or archaeology or particle physics. That is to say, there are ascending levels of practice. In any field, the key to mastery is always the same: practice, practice, practice. Ask any musician. In *Outliers*, Malcolm Gladwell surfaces some interesting data suggesting that the difference between someone who is great at a certain activity and someone who is only good at it is that the star performer has chalked up no less than ten thousand hours of practice. That sounds about right to me. What's that? You're scared by the notion that you have to put in ten thousand hours to get great at this Active Dreaming? Relax: you can practice every night and every day, and those hours will mount up fast. It won't feel one bit like "work," because you'll find it wonderful fun, constantly energizing, and capable of putting a champagne fizz of excitement and entertainment in the air in any environment whatsoever. And you are ready to start today, because the time is actually always Now and you have the material and the opportunity.

Active Dreaming offers three core areas of practice.

First, Active Dreaming is a way of *talking and walking our dreams*, of bringing energy and guidance from the dreamworld into everyday life. We learn how to create a safe space where we can share dreams of the night and dreams of life with others, receive helpful feedback, and encourage one another to take creative and healing action. We discover that each of us can play guide for others, and that by sharing in the right way we claim our voices, grow our power as storytellers and communicators, build stronger friendships, and lay foundations for a new kind of community. Indigenous dreamers maintain, wisely, that if we don't *do* something with our dreams, we do not dream well.

Second, Active Dreaming is a method of *shamanic lucid dreaming*. It starts with simple, everyday practice and extends to profound group experiences of time travel, soul recovery, and the exploration of multidimensional reality. It is founded on the understanding that we don't need to go to sleep in order to dream. The easiest way to become a conscious or lucid dreamer is to start out lucid and stay that way. As a method of conscious dream navigation, Active Dreaming is not to be confused with approaches that purport to "control" or manipulate dreams; it is utterly misguided to seek to put the control freak that is the ego in charge of something immeasurably wiser and deeper than itself.

Third, Active Dreaming is a way of conscious *living*. This requires us to reclaim our inner child and the child's gift of spontaneity, play, and imagination. It requires us to claim the power of naming and to define our life project. It invites us to discover and follow the natural path of our energies. It calls us to remember our bigger and braver story and tell and live it in such a way that it can be heard and received by others. It is about walking in everyday life as if we are moving through a forest of living symbols that are looking at us (to borrow from Baudelaire, who saw these things with a poet's clarity). It is about navigating by synchronicity and receiving the chance events and symbolic pop-ups on our daily roads as clues to a deeper order. Beyond this, it is about grasping that the energy we carry and the attitudes we choose (consciously or unconsciously) have a magnetic effect on the world around us, drawing or repelling encounters and circumstances. When we rise to this perspective, we are able to welcome the things that block or oppose us as opportunities for course correction or as tests that will confirm us in our calling if we are willing to develop the courage and clarity to pursue it.

As Stephen Nachmanovitch writes in *Free Play*, "we can depend on the world being a perpetual surprise in perpetual motion. And a perpetual invitation to create." To live consciously is to accept the challenge to create, which is to move beyond scripts and bring something new into the world.

IN PART 3 OF THIS BOOK, we'll learn that this approach is not only for individuals and friends and families but also for communities, and that it will stimulate our deeper attunement to the cause of the earth. Active dreamers become Speakers for the earth and rise to full awareness of the truth of the indigenous wisdom that tells us we must be mindful of the consequences of our actions on others, down to the seventh generation beyond ourselves. Active dream groups can offer a model of intentional community and can foster a new mode of leadership devoted to empowering each member to claim her voice and play guide to others as they learn to speak and embody their own truth.

In the appendix, we'll study documents from a possible future in which a Commonwealth of Dreamers has emerged, guided by priestess-scientists who are applying the gifts of dreaming to mend our world.

PART 1

Wake Up and Dream

Dreams are the guiding words of the soul.

— CARL JUNG, *The Red Book*

1

Punch a Hole in the World

The child's psyche is of infinite extent and incalculable age.

— CARL JUNG, "The Development of Personality"

To understand dreams and reclaim the practice of imagination, we must look to the master teachers: our inner children and the children around us. When very young, children know how to go to magic kingdoms without paying for tickets, because they are at home in the imagination and live close to their dreams. When she was four years old, my daughter Sophie had adventures in a special place called Teddy Bear Land, where she met a special friend. I loved hearing about these travels and encouraged her to make drawings and spin further stories from them.

One day Sophie sat down beside me and asked with great earnestness, "Daddy, would you like to know how I get to Teddy Bear Land?"

"I'd love to."

"Sometimes I take the Sun Gate. Sometimes I take the Moon Gate. Sometimes I take the Tree Gate. Sometimes I take the Rainbow Bridge. And *sometimes* I just punch a hole in the world."

I've never heard anyone say it better. To live the larger life, we need to *punch a hole in the world.* This is what dreaming — whether we are sleeping or waking or hyperawake — is really all about. On our roads to adulthood, we sometimes forget how to do it, just as older children in the *Chronicles of Narnia* cease to be able to see Aslan as they approach adolescence and become more and more burdened by the reality definitions of the grown-ups around them.

When we listen, truly listen, to very young children, we start to remember that the distance between us and the magic kingdoms is no wider than the edge of a sleep mask. True listening requires us to pay attention. To *attend,* according to its root meaning in the Latin, is to stretch ourselves, which requires us to expand our vocabulary of understanding. We owe nothing less to the young children in our lives. When we do this, we discover that they can be our very best teachers of how to dream and what dreaming can be.

What to Do When You're Eaten by a T-Rex

"I was eaten by T-Rex." Brian, aged seven, is rocking in his seat with excitement, but his voice is very soft. The fifteen kids in the circle, plus parents and grandparents, lean forward to hear him. We've gathered to spend a half day together at a local retreat center for a playshop I love to lead called Dreaming with Children and Families.

"Did T-Rex swallow you in one gulp?" Brian's grandmother asks, making a gurgling in her throat as she mimics something very big taking a big gulp. "Or did he kind of munch on you?"

"It was a *big* gulp." Brian's eyes are gleaming with excitement. "Then I was falling down, down into T-Rex's belly. I found two eggs. I cut them open and there were two baby T-Rexes inside. They came out and they killed the big T-Rex and I was fine."

"How did you feel?" I ask.

"*Grrreat!*"

You don't analyze a dream like this, whatever the age of the dreamer — at least not until you do something to grab the vital energy of the dream and embody it and bring it through to the present. This isn't hard with Brian's dream. We have a room full of excited kids, and kids are naturals for dream theater.

"Hey, Brian, would you like to playact your dream?"

Brian can't wait. He chooses the two youngest children in the group, an angelic four-year-old named Abby who has just created a picture of one of her own dreams with crayons and sketch paper — a picture of a wild thing she has given her own name — and a toddler who has proved a virtuoso with maracas and other noisemakers from our communal music box.

"Aunt" Carol, our host at the retreat center and a gifted counselor and dream teacher, is picked to play the snapping head of T-Rex, a tricky role since she can't stop beaming and laughing. There are plenty of dreamers, kids of all ages, to make up the body and tail of the beast. Soon the monster we've made is roaring and thumping around the room. Brian, playing himself, darts around, trying to hide behind the furniture; his fate is preordained. He is swallowed by T-Rex. He rolls over and over, playacting his descent into the belly of the beast. Way down deep inside, he finds the eggs and frees the baby monsters, who return the favor by saving him.

This is wild and happy and just-so, and everybody wants more.

We turn other kids' dreams into theater, and each time a new strategy emerges for dealing with dream monsters. A ten-year-old girl tells us a dream in which she's at school, on her way to lunch, when a "short monster" appears and starts eating her classmates. "He couldn't eat me, because I kicked him in the face."

Playacting that one produces a stampede as a very small boy, thrilled to be playing the short monster, pursues the dreamer's classmates until he is laid flat by a pretend kick to his face. Everyone laughs as the dreamer dabs at the slime the short monster has left on her foot.

A thirteen-year-old girl in the group is menaced in her dream by people behaving like monsters. She puts on bat wings and flies off to a special place where she can be safe. The scariest adults in the dream are the ones who remain strangely frozen, as if they have been encased in blocks of ice, while she tries to avoid the attackers. In a later scene, she is at a wild ocean. When she plunges in, she becomes a killer whale and swims with delight with an orca friend who comes to join her. When she shape-shifts back into the form of a teenage girl, the grown-ups are no longer a threat to her. She has brought power back from the place of the killer whales.

THESE ARE SCENES FROM A SINGLE AFTERNOON of dreaming with kids and their families, the way our ancestors used to do it and some indigenous peoples still do. We had started out right, by drumming and making cheerful music to call up the dreams that wanted to play with us. Then everyone grabbed art supplies from the center of the circle to make a drawing of a dream.

Also at the center of the room, we had placed a huge toy box full of stuffed animals and puppets and plastic lizards. I invited the kids to grab any animal they liked. Then, since we were on traditional Mohawk Indian land, I had them join hands and voices in singing a simple Mohawk song that calls in the Bear — and with it, all of the other animals — as helpers and protectors.

> Don't cry, little one.
> Don't cry, little one.
> The Bear is coming to dance for you.
> The Bear is coming to dance for you.

We discussed how, if you have a scary dream, it's good to know you have a friend who can help you out and take care of you. Little Abby came over to me and whispered confidentially, "I have a bear. And I have lots of dream friends."

We broke every half hour for snacks of orange slices and chocolate chip cookies.

Toward the end, I opened my dream journal to a page where I had drawn a picture of Champie — the cousin of the Loch Ness monster who reputedly lives in Lake Champlain — swimming in the East River in front of the island of Manhattan, with delighted kids riding on his back. This was an image that had come to me spontaneously in a recent drumming circle.

I told the kids and their parents and grandparents: "A journal like this, where you draw your dreams and write down your stories, is a treasure book. I hope everyone here will now start keeping a treasure book. Ask the grown-ups who brought you to help you find the right one. They can help you write down the words if you like. But there's one thing about a dream journal everyone should know. It's your special book, and if you don't want Mommy or Daddy to read it, you should tell them: 'This is my secret book.' And they must respect that."

I asked if there were any questions.

Hands went up all around the room.

"Can we do this again?"

"Can we do it every month?"

"Can we do it every *week*?"

"Hey," I responded, "you can do it every *day* at home or at a friend's house now that you and your families know how much fun it is."

When Kids Dream the Future

Children don't have to be told that we are all psychics in our dreams. They know this, because they have psychic experiences in their dreams all the time. They see into the future, they encounter the departed, they see things happening at a distance and behind doors that are supposedly locked against them. The problem is that very often the adults around them won't listen, sometimes because they are afraid of what the child may be seeing.

I once led a series of dream classes for sixth-grade schoolchildren as part of a "talented and gifted" program in a school district in upstate New York. At the start of each class, one of the questions I put to the kids was: "Has anyone dreamed something that later happened?" On average, nine out of ten kids said they had had this experience. A tough young boy who looked like Rambo in the making shot up his arm, eager to tell his story. "We went on family vacation in Myrtle Beach. I dreamed the whole ride from the airport, turn by turn. I kept trying to tell Dad which way to go, but he wouldn't listen to me. So we spent an hour getting lost and doubling back, because Dad doesn't believe in dreams."

My friend Wanda Burch, the author of *She Who Dreams*, remembers what her son Evan saw in a dream when he was just three years old. Although this is a family of dreamers, the parents did not understand the dream until it began to play out in waking life — at which point the dream prompted the quick action that may have saved mother and child from serious injury. Here's how Wanda told me the story that unfolded at their home in the Mohawk Valley of New York:

My son was just a bit over three years old and already sharing great dreams. He told me he had dreamed about "the dogs" and was terribly frightened of the dream, but seemed unable to express why they terrified him so much. My husband was working very hard and was really exhausted on the evening of a board meeting, so I offered to drive him the fifteen miles from our home in the Mohawk Valley.

Just as we closed the door of the house, Evan began screaming, "The dogs, the dogs!," pulling on my hands. I had to pick him up to get him in the car, and told him over and over again there were no dogs. He calmed down. When we dropped off my husband and prepared to drive home, Evan got agitated again, looking out the back window and telling me there were growling dogs. We spent a few minutes discussing nightmares and things he could do with the dream in order to work with it. I don't recall what I told him at that time, but he was usually quite capable of dreaming his own solutions to his nightmares, so I was surprised this one was scaring him so much.

We drove back home. The same scenario began again. I had to carry Evan into the house. This time he was screaming so hysterically I could barely pick him up. He calmed down again in the house. Time to pick up my husband. Again, Evan was hysterical, thrashing around in a desperate attempt to avoid getting in the car.

When we returned to our home with my husband, Evan started screaming. I was struggling to get him from the car to the house. When we were just feet away from the glass-enclosed porch, I heard the most terrifying barking and growling. I turned in that instant to see a pack of wild dogs coming over a slight rise just yards away from the cottage. I literally threw Evan into the porch, screaming at my husband to close the door and stay in the car. I barely made it through the door to slam it against several of the dogs as their bodies lunged against the porch. Several crashed against the door and walls of the enclosed porch before they whirled around and ran off with the pack.

If I had not been able to throw Evan into the porch and my-self after him, we would have been in serious trouble. At this point, my son was completely calm, staring out the window at the dogs as they vanished into the creek bed. He looked at me and said, "The dogs!" I said to him, "Yes, I got it."

My son has shared his dreams, big and small, with me all his life — and still does, now that he is in his late thirties. I turned to him in my darkest moments when I was experienc-ing doubts about my ability to heal from a life-threatening ill-ness. I asked him, "Am I okay? What are you dreaming?" I'll never forget his response: "You are fine. I am dreaming you into the future."

If you have any doubts about our ability to dream the future — and to use our night previews of possible future events to make better choices and change things for the better — listen to a young child telling his or her dreams. And consider how *you* may be required to recognize and act on clues to the possible future contained in the dream you are hearing. To put it mildly, children are not independent players on the stage of life. They need us not only to listen but to help.

I once led a dreamplay session for a group of at-risk inner-city kids in New Haven, Connecticut, hosted by the local Police Benevolent As-sociation. A beautiful fourteen-year-old girl told a dream in which she gets off a bus on a winding mountain road and is attacked by two wild dogs with red eyes. The dogs didn't sound like regular dogs, but the de-scription of the rest stop on the mountain road was very literal and spe-cific, though she said she'd never been to a place like that in regular life. We were lucky that day to have a counselor in the room who recognized the dream locale. "She has just described a rest stop on the road we'll be taking to summer camp in a couple of weeks. I'll be on that bus, and I promise you nothing bad is gonna happen at that stop, because I'll be there to make sure of that."

Helping Kids to Make a Secret Book

Luca had not yet turned four when he climbed into his mom's bed in the middle of the night and told her the following dream:

> I was running away from a huge T-Rex who was chasing me. Then I remembered, "Wait a minute, I like T-Rex." So I turned around and told him, "Hey, you're my favorite dinosaur!" And he picked me up so I could ride, and then we went to the beach together.

In the morning, Luca asked his mother to write the dream down for him. Luca did something inside his dream we all want to learn to do. Instead of running away from something scary, he turned around and faced it, on its own ground. Luca's mom did the essential first thing that adults need to do with kids' dreams: she *listened*. At Luca's instigation, she then did the next most important thing: she helped her young child to *do something fun* with a dream, which in this case simply meant writing it down so the story would be a keeper.

Luca often told his dreams to his Aunt Chele, an active dreamer who had been keeping a dream journal for many years. Inspired by Aunt Chele's example of writing her dreams in her journal, Luca's mom provided Luca with the most special book any of us will ever have — a book filled with the magic of our dreams and imagination. If we are privileged to have access to young children, one of the greatest gifts we can give them — and in the process, ourselves — is to encourage them to record dreams and stories in a book that will become a journal. I did this with my own daughters. When they were very young, they would do the pictures and I would write the words for them. They took over more and more of the writing as they got older, until, at age nine, they were keeping their journals by themselves and for themselves. Then the same thing happened in each case. They said to me, in effect: "That's it, Dad. This is my secret book, and you can't read it anymore."

Now *that's* a journal. The secret book of your Self, not to be shared with anyone without permission, which should not be given lightly.

Nine Keys to Helping Kids with Their Dreams

Here's what we need to know about listening to children's dreams and supporting their imaginations:

1. *Listen up!* When a child wants to tell a dream, make room for that. Make some daily space for dream sharing. Listen to the stories and cherish them for their own sake.

2. *Invite good dreams.* Pick the right bedtime reading or, better still, tell stories. Help your child weave a web of good dream intentions for the night — for example, by asking, "What would you most like to do tonight?" Encourage children to sleep with a favorite stuffed animal (whether teddy bear or T-Rex) and make this a dream guardian.

3. *Provide immediate help with the scary stuff.* If your child was scared by something in the night, recognize that *you* are the ally the child needs right now. Do something right away to clear out that negative energy. Get a frightened child to spit it out (literally) or draw a picture of what scared her and tear it up as violently as possible.

4. *Ask good questions.* When the child has told her story, ask good questions. Ask about feelings, the color of the sky, and exactly what T-Rex was doing. See if there's something about the future. Say what you would think about it if this were your dream. Always come up with something fun or helpful to do with this story. Open up the crayon box, call Grandma, and so on.

5. *Help the child to keep a dream journal.* Get this started as early as possible. With a very young child, you can help with the words while she does the pictures. When your child reaches the point where she closes the journal and says, "This is my secret book, and you can't read it anymore," *do not peek.* Give her privacy, and let her choose when she'll let you look in that magic book.

6. *Provide tools for creative expression.* Encourage the child to bring dreams alive through art, dance, theater, and games and to draw or paint dreams. Gather friends and family for dream-inspired games and performance. Puppets and stuffed animals can be great for acting out dreams. This can also be dress-up time. It's such a release for kids to portray Mom or Dad or other grownups in their lives — be ready to be shocked!

7. *Help construct effective action plans.* Dreams can show us things

that require further action — for example, to avoid an unhappy future event that was previewed in the dream, or to put something right in a family situation. A child will probably need adult help with such things, starting with your help. This will require you to learn more about dreaming and dreamwork, as you are doing now.

8. *Let your own inner child out to play.* As you listen to children's dreams, let the wonderful child dreamer inside you come out and join in the play.

9. *Keep it fun!* When you get the hang of this, you'll find it's the best home entertainment you can enjoy.

Notice two things that are not on this list but that would be at the very top of a list of what *not* to do with a child's dreams:

1. *Never* say to a child: "It's only a dream." Children know that dreams are for real, and that the scary stuff that comes out in dreams needs to be resolved, not dismissed.

2. *Do* NOT *interpret* a child's dreams. You're not the expert here; the child is.

2

How to Break a Dream Drought

Those who lose the Dreaming are lost.

— AUSTRALIAN ABORIGINAL SAYING

Too many of us have lost touch with our dreams. It's no exaggeration to state that our society is suffering a severe and protracted dream drought.

From the viewpoint of many spiritual traditions, this is a very serious condition. It's through dreams, say the Navajo, that humans keep in touch with the spirit realm. If you have lost your dreams, say the Iroquois, you've lost part of your soul. "It is an age-old fact," declared the great psychologist C. G. Jung in his last major essay, "that God speaks chiefly through dreams and visions."[1]

There are three main reasons for the dream drought in many modern lives:

1. *Bad habits.* The rhythms and routines of a typical urban life simply don't support dream recall. Too often we are jolted awake by alarm clocks — or bedmates, or kids who need to get to school — and stumble out into the world, fueled with caffeine, to try to get through our rounds of deadlines and obligations.

In many situations, we have nothing that supports and rewards the habit of taking time to collect our dreams. Most of us also lack a practice for creating a safe space where we can share our dreams, receive helpful feedback, and be supported in devising creative action to embody the guidance and energy of our dreams. If we don't do something with our dreams, we will not dream well.

2. *Fear and regret.* We run away from our dreams because we think they might be telling us something we don't want to hear — about the dark side of ourselves, or trouble or illness ahead. We slam the door and say, "It's only a dream." This is a poor strategy. Issues we leave unresolved in the night are likely to come round and bite us in the rear end in the everyday world.

   Alternatively, we dream of something wonderful — of joy and delight with Mr. or Ms. Right, of a dream home, a dream job, a world of peace and beauty. But when we wake up, we tell ourselves there's no one like Mr. Right in our life, or we don't have the looks or the money or the ability to manifest what we enjoyed in our dreams. So again we kiss off the dreams, telling ourselves they are "only" dreams. Again, this is a foolish reflex. If we can dream it, we may just be able to do it.

3. *Artificial sleep cycles.* Very often our concept of a good night's sleep is at odds with our dreams. Many of us believe — supported by any number of sleep doctors and pharmaceutical companies — that we need to spend seven or eight hours each night in uninterrupted sleep. This idea would have amazed our ancestors. Before the advent of artificial lighting (gas and then electricity), most humans experienced "segmented sleep," divided into at least two distinct cycles, a "first sleep" and a "second sleep," as they used to be called in England.

   Experiments by a team led by Dr. Thomas Wehr for the National Institute of Mental Health suggest that, deprived of artificial lighting, people revert to the ancient sleep plan, with an interval of several hours between the two sleeps. One of the most interesting findings of Wehr's research is that, during this interval, subjects typically register elevated levels of prolactin, a pituitary hormone that helps hens to brood peacefully on their eggs for prolonged periods and assists humans in laying eggs of a different kind, by putting them into a benign, altered state of consciousness not unlike meditation.[2] Sleep historian A. Roger Ekirch says flatly, "Consolidated sleep, as we experience it today, is unnatural."[3]

Among indigenous and early peoples, the liminal state of *dorveille* (sleep-wake) is a time when you might stir and share dreams with whoever is available. It's a highly creative state, so much so that, in my *Secret History of Dreaming*, I have called it the "solution state," based on the many scientific discoveries and other breakthroughs that have come to people while in this zone. When we are primed or medicated to give ourselves just one longish sleep period, we limit our chances of recalling and sharing dreams, and we deprive ourselves of easy access to the fertile field of hypnagogia — the images that come and the connections that are made — between sleep and waking.

Five Ways to Break a Dream Drought

Have you lost touch with your dreams? Is your dream recall limited to fragments that fade away as you hurry off into the business and traffic of the day? Relax. Here are some fun and easy ways to renew and refresh your relationship with your dreams.

1. *Set an intention for the night.* Before sleep, write down an intention for the hours of dream and twilight that lie ahead. This can be a travel plan ("I would like to go to Hawaii" or "I would like to visit my girlfriend/boyfriend"). It might be a specific request for guidance ("I want to know what will happen if I change my job"). It could be a more general setting of direction ("I ask for healing" or "I open myself to my creative source"). You might simply say, "I want to have fun in my dreams and remember."

    Make sure your intention has some *juice*. Don't make dream recall one more chore to fit in with all the others.

If you like, you can make a little ritual of dream incubation, a simple version of what ancient seekers did when they traveled to temples of dream healing, like those of Asklepios, in hopes of a night encounter with a sacred guide. You can take a special bath or shower, play a recording of the sounds of nature or running water, and meditate for a while on an object or picture that relates to your intention. You might want to avoid eating heavily or drinking alcohol within a couple of hours of sleep. You could get yourself a little mugwort pillow — in folk tradition, mugwort is an excellent dream bringer — and place it under or near your regular pillow.

2. *Be ready to receive.* Having set your intention, make sure you have the means to honor it. Keep pen and paper (or a voice recorder) next to your bed so you are ready to record when you wake up. Record *something* whenever you wake up, even if it's at 3 AM. If you have to go to the bathroom, take your notebook with you and practice doing two things at once. Sometimes the dreams we most need to hear come visiting at rather antisocial hours, from the viewpoint of the little, everyday mind.

3. *Be kind to fragments.* Don't give up on fragments from your night dreams. The wispiest trace of a dream can be exciting to play with, and as you play with it you may find you pull back more of the previously forgotten dream. The odd word or phrase left over from a dream may be an intriguing clue, if you are willing to do a little detective work.

Suppose you wake with nothing more than the sense of a certain color. It could be interesting to notice that today is a Red Day, or a Green Day, to dress accordingly, to allow the energy of that color to travel with you, and to meditate on the qualities of red or green and see what life memories that evokes.

4. *Still no dream recall? No worries.* If you don't remember a dream when you first wake up, laze in bed for a few minutes and see if something comes back. Wiggle around in the bed. Sometimes returning to the body posture we were in earlier in the night

helps to bring back what we were dreaming when we were in that position.

If you still don't have a dream, write something down anyway: whatever is in your awareness, including feelings and physical sensations. You are catching the residue of a dream even if the dream itself is gone. As you do this, you are saying to the source of your dreams: "I'm listening. Talk to me."

You may find that, though your dreams have flown, you have a sense of clarity and direction that is a legacy of the night. We solve problems in our sleep even when we don't remember the problem-solving process that went on in our dreaming minds.

5. *Remember, you don't need to go to sleep in order to dream.* The incidents of everyday life will speak to us like dream symbols if we are willing to pay attention. Keep a lookout for the first unusual or striking thing that enters your field of perception in the course of the day, and ask whether there could be a message there. Sometimes it's in your face, as happened to a woman I know who was mourning the end of a romance but had to laugh when she noticed that the bumper sticker on the red convertible in front of her said, "I use ex-lovers as speed bumps."

When we make it our game to pay attention to coincidence and symbolic pop-ups in everyday life, we oil the dream gates so they let more through from the night. This happened to a woman who came to a series of evening dream classes I was leading. She told us: "I've come to break a dream drought." She thought she knew why she was missing her dreams. "I'm scared my dreams are telling me that I'm going to lose my job."

I suggested that, since she'd had no recent dreams, she might want to let the world speak to her in the manner of a dream by carrying a question with her into the night and receiving the first unusual thing that happened as a personal response from the universe. She wrote down the question "Is my job okay?"

We were eager to hear her report at the next class. She told us she got her message right away. "Although I know the neighborhood well,

I found myself driving the wrong way down a one-way street — and didn't notice until a big truck threatened to push me off the road. I guess I'd better start looking for a new job."

After this incident, she started recalling dreams again and had several to share in the new class. She had dreamed she was in Washington, D.C., at a conference on transportation. As we explored this dream, she revealed that her current work consisted mostly of arranging conferences, and that she had a friend in Washington. "But I know nothing about transportation — except maybe how to drive the wrong way down a one-way street."

We need to *do* something with our dreams. By the end of that class, the dreamer had developed a clear action plan. She would use frequent-flier miles to visit her friend and would check out job opportunities in the D.C. area. She made that trip and quickly found a new job. Six months later, her former department was terminated. She was now happily resettled in Washington, earning 50 percent more money in her new job — which included arranging the conference on transportation she had dreamed.

Dreaming is not only about soul; it's also about keeping body and soul together. Dreaming is one of the vital resources that help us get through life's obstacle course.

Are you feeling wistful about the dreams you've missed? There are places we can go to look for lost dreams.

The Office of Lost and Found Dreams

What happens to the dreams we don't remember?

I've asked myself that question on several mornings when I've awoken with little or no dream recall while feeling that the night had been active.

On one such morning, I decided to linger in bed and see whether I could find a place where I could recover lost dreams. I found myself approaching an old-time cinema that reminded me of a movie theater where I used to go as a boy to watch Saturday matinees. I was amazed and delighted to find that, this time, the movie titles on the marquee and the images on the posters in the lobby all throbbed with significance in my present life.

Waking the Sleeping King was blazoned in lights.

One of the posters showed a boy riding a monster of the deep through a stormy ocean. Another depicted a steamy romance. The girl at the ticket kiosk smiled and gestured for me to go through. Soon I was settled in a comfy, padded velvet seat in a private screening room. As dream images filled the screen, I realized I had a choice. I could remain a comfortable observer, or I could enter the fray.

On another morning, after coffee, I decided to try the same method again. This time, instead of going back to the movie house, I found myself drawn to the kind of video store that is almost defunct, thanks to our new instant-delivery systems. This video store was vast, with its products arranged on many levels, On the first floor, dreams were arranged like DVDs on shelves according to familiar categories — drama, comedy, family, and so on. There was a large adult section, most of whose content was unfamiliar to me. I realized that a block had been placed on some of this material so that it did not reach my conscious mind, or — in cases where the film had been rated I (for *intrusion*) — had not been allowed through during the night.

I discovered sections devoted to my dreams of individual people. I had only to focus on a name or title, and the movie began to play all around me, so I could enter it at will.

On a lower level of the dream video store, I discovered that I could explore dream adventures I may have shared with other people but had not remembered. I found an immense archive of shared dreams involving each of these people. One archive was as large as a Gothic cathedral, with shelves rising to the high ceiling many stories above. I watched several dream movies in each location. They took me deeply and vividly into scenes of other lives and other times — of leopard people in Africa, of Celtic voyagers in a coracle on a cold northern sea, of a turning castle in a high desert landscape where everything was the color of sand except for the pretty star-shaped flowers, blue and purple, on a terrace. The dream movies revealed a hidden order of connection in all these relationships that transcended our present lives.

On yet another day, when I felt impelled to go searching for lost dreams, I was drawn to a building that looked like an old-fashioned post office. It resembled the post office in the Rust Belt city of Troy, New York, where I once lived. When I arrived in front of it, in my conscious dream, the sky turned dark. I mounted the high steps and walked past the mailboxes toward the counters. Most of the steel shutters were down and locked for the night, but one was still half-open. Behind it, I saw letters spilling from pigeonholes and heaps of giant mailbags and packages. A small black woman in a blue uniform hurried to the desk and handed me a letter. I was moved to tears when I opened it and found a message from a beloved family member, long deceased.

When I turned to thank the postal clerk, I realized that I knew her. I had glimpsed her, in half-forgotten dreams, slipping mail through a letter drop in the door of my house, a letter drop that is not in the physical door. She strongly resembles a figure from history I was called to study by dreams I *did* remember — Harriet Tubman, a world-class dreamer who used her visions as maps to guide escaping slaves to freedom on the Underground Railroad before the American Civil War.

I suspect there are back rooms in my dream post office where there is more to discover. Maybe one of them is like the *cabinet noir* in the old French post offices, where mail judged suspect by the authorities was held for inspection and often was never delivered to the addressee.

If you are missing your dreams (and your dreams are missing you), try taking a little quiet time, when you won't be disturbed, and announce this as your intention: "I would like to go to a place where I can find my lost dreams."

Maybe this will take you to a movie theater, a video store, or a post office, or another place entirely, constructed from your own life memories and suited to your imagination. Whatever form it takes, you will be entering the Office of Lost and Found Dreams.

3

Talking and Walking Our Dreams

You are never given a dream without also being given the power
to make it true. You may have to work for it, however.

— RICHARD BACH

U nless we do something with our dreams, we will not dream well.
This is indigenous wisdom, understood by all of our ancestors
when they lived in cultures that valued dreams and the dreamer. As my
friends of the Six Nations tell it, soul speaks to us in dreams, showing
us what it desires. If we do not take action to honor such dreams, soul
becomes disgusted with us and withdraws its energy and vitality from
our lives.

Dreaming is making a comeback in our modern world. Dream
groups are sprouting up everywhere, to the point where the *New York
Times* has dubbed them "the new book clubs."[4] Hardheads in the media
are slowly opening to the discussion of dreams as something more than
random neuronal firing in the brain or Freudian smutty jokes.

But there is a simple and essential principle that we must follow if
we are to get good at dreaming again and allow our dreams to be good
to us. *Dreams require action* — action to embody their energy and guidance and to bring it into our everyday lives and the lives of those around

us. My Active Dreaming approach, which now guides dream groups and individual dreamers all over the world, upholds the principle that every dreamwork practice must result in an action plan. We are not content with some nebulous wishy-washy statement of general intention or spiritual correctness, such as "I'll meditate more." We want specific, practical action of the kind that both entertains the soul and sustains the body.

Of course, dreams can be mysterious and hard to relate to the issues of everyday life. In one of his seminars on dreams from childhood, Jung remarked that dreams "fall like nuts from the tree of life, and yet they are so hard to crack."[5] So the first action we may need to take is to find the right kind of nutcracker.

We don't have to seek this alone. Once we learn to share our dreams *in the right way* with a partner or a group, we have an excellent recourse both for understanding our dreams and for determining the right action to honor them.

Lightning Dreamwork is an original and powerful process that I developed after observing that previous methods of dream sharing and dream analysis just weren't enough fun and were short on action.

One of the great contributions of the American dreamwork movement has been to insist that *dreams belong to the dreamers.* As Henry Reed, a PhD in psychology and one of the founders of the movement, likes to say, "Dreaming is too important to be left to psychologists." Montague ("Monte") Ullman, a clinical psychiatrist, made an enormous personal contribution when he declared that none of us have the right to tell another person what his or her dream means based on certification or presumed authority. In commenting on one another's dreams, we should begin by saying, "If it were my dream," making it clear that we are offering our personal associations and projections, not presuming to tell the dreamer the definitive meaning of his or her dream. The work and example of Henry Reed, Monte Ullman, Jeremy Taylor, and grassroots dreamwork circles all over the United States helped to return dreams to the dreamers, affirming that we don't need to be doctors or shrinks to offer helpful comments on someone else's dreams. "Perhaps the most significant development concerning dreams in the latter decades of the twentieth century is returning them to their rightful owner, the dreamer," says Reed,[6] and I agree.

But more was required. Dream sharing needs to be fast enough to suit our busy schedules and Western hurry-sickness, and so fun and so helpful that people will want to do it as often as possible. Every dream-work process — whether five minutes by the office coffee machine or in a dedicated dream group or workshop — needs to become an *energy event* that delivers juice as well as information. We want to bring energy as well as content from the place of dreaming, and we want to get that energy moving in the room and traveling beyond the room at the end of a conversation or session.

Playing the Lightning Dreamwork Game

Building on the foundations laid by America's dreamwork pioneers, I invented a simple, high-octane process for sharing dreams with a partner or a group that I dubbed Lightning Dreamwork because it is meant to be fast (it can be done in five minutes) and to focus energy, like a lightning strike.

It has four steps. Step 1 is to get the dreamer to tell her story as simply and clearly as possible, leaving out autobiography and explanations. Stories need titles, so the dreamer should be encouraged to come up with a title for her dream report. In this way, the dreamer is helped to claim the power of creating and telling stories, which is central to the art of conscious living. When we can tell our story in a way that others can hear and receive, we have acquired real power that can be applied to any situation, from ending a family drama to winning a new job or a book contract.

In step 2, the person who is hearing the dream asks a few questions to get the bare minimum of facts required to place the dream in a context and see how it may apply to the rest of the dreamer's life, past, present, and future. The first question is always about feelings. How you feel immediately after a dream is the first and best guide to the nature of the dream. The next questions involve running a reality check on the dream. What does the dreamer recognize from her dream in the rest of her life? And is it remotely possible that any part of this dream could play out in the future, either literally or symbolically? I also like to ask the dreamer: What do you want to know about this dream?

Step 3 is to play the If It Were My Dream game. Anyone present during the telling of the dream gets to play. If you are commenting on someone else's dream, you can do no wrong as long as you follow the simple rule of prefacing your opinions and associations by saying, "If it were my dream..." You are not allowed to interpret another person's dream. You are going to pretend that her dream is your dream and talk about whatever comes to mind when you play that role, which might range from dreams of your own with a similar theme to your feelings about spiders and the one you found spinning a web over your bed.

Step 4 is to get the dreamer to come up with an action plan, by which I mean a specific and practical way to honor the dream. Sometimes even veteran dreamers are clueless when asked for an action plan. So in a Lightning Dreamwork session, we are all poised to make suggestions about how to move beyond talking to walking a dream.

On the way to an action plan, we ask the dreamer to come up with what Mark Twain called a "snapper," a personal catchphrase that captures the essence of the dream and the insights that have come through in discussion. This is a neat way to retain a message, and it orients us toward doing something about it.

Come up with the right snapper, and it may lead you to the right snap decision.

I'm a Real Fox

Here's an example of Lightning Dreamwork as informal everyday practice. A neighbor who works in state government stopped me on the street when I was walking my dog. John wanted to know if it would be okay for him to share a dream with me. I invited him to meet me at my house when my dog had done his business. Twenty minutes later, he told me the following dream:

> I have taken on the role of a very important man. I have to find something of tremendous importance. I can't get to it until the earth opens, and I am hurled into a kind of primal experience

of earth changes over millions of years. I watch mountains rise and fall, and oceans grow and recede. I am in the magma of the living planet.

I find what I'm seeking. It's doesn't look like all that much. It's an animal skull, not that big.

Then I'm back in the house as the important man. People jump to follow my orders. I tell them I know where exactly to dig. I point to the spot in the yard. They start digging, but their tools are no good. I tell them to go get better tools to do the job right.

I asked John the essential first question: How did you feel when you woke up? He said he didn't want to leave the dream. He was having such a good time. He felt powerful and on track.

While running the reality check, he said he didn't feel very powerful at work. His boss was unpredictable, and he sometimes felt vulnerable. He wanted to know how he could embody the sense of power he found in the dream.

I told him that — if it were my dream — I might think it was coaching me to take on a more important role in my work. He allowed that this was a distinct possibility. I remarked that I'd draw from the dream the practical counsel that I might need to bring other people along. The big thing that struck me was how, in the dream, my neighbor felt closely connected to primal energy, to earth changes — and I added that I would want, in whatever I chose to do, to bring that energy and connectedness to bear in my life.

He vigorously agreed. "That's what I want to do. I feel I need that connection to feed my soul."

I was intrigued by the animal skull. What kind of animal was it? "Maybe a dog or fox."

I got goose bumps, because when he was recounting the dream I had had the distinct impression of a fox. I talked about the fox as a shamanic ally in the oldest shamanic traditions of Europe, and about the nature of the fox as an animal legendary for its cunning, required to know when to hunt and when to hide — renowned, of course, as a trickster.

John teared up. He explained that he had recently done his turn-of-the-year personal reading of the I Ching. He had cast the last hexagram, named "Before Completion." The judgment evokes the need for extreme caution, to act as a wily old fox on thin ice, not as a young fox that might fall through the cracks.

I suggested that, in any future work dramas, I would pause to ask, "What would the wily old fox do?" before adopting any course of action.

He grinned when he came up with a bumper sticker that he could use, "I'm a real fox." He said he would honor his dream and keep in touch with its energy by putting a small figure of a fox on his bureaucrat's desk.

The conversation juiced both of us. Everyday dreamwork is soul food for everyone involved.

EXERCISE FOR PARTNERS OR GROUPS

Playing the Lightning Dreamwork Game

Step One: Tell the Dream

1. Choose who will tell a dream first.
2. Encourage the dreamer to tell the dream as clearly and simply as possible, without personal background or analysis.
3. Ask the dreamer to give the dream a title.

Step Two: Ask Three Essential Questions

The partner (or lead partner, if working in a group) now asks the dreamer three basic questions.

1. What did you feel when you woke up?
2. The reality check question, which has two critical aspects:
   - Do you recognize any of the people or situations of the dream in waking life?
   - Could any part of this dream be played out in waking life in the future?
3. What would you like to know about this dream?

Step Three: Play the "If It Were My Dream" Game

The partner now says to the dreamer: "If it were my dream, I would think about such and such." You can say anything you like, as long as you say it politely! You may find that your own dreams or life memories come to mind in the presence of another person's dream, and these may be your way of understanding some part of the other's experience. You can mention those personal memories by saying, "If it were my dream, I would think about my other dreams of a house that has a mystery in the basement (or an extra story)."

Step Four: Honor the Dream

Dreams require action! The vital last part of the process requires the partner to ask the dreamer:

- What action will you take to honor this dream?

    Try to guide the dreamer toward specific *action*. If the dreamer does not know what to do, the partner should suggest possible actions he would take if it were his dream. Some suggestions:

- Write a bumper sticker or "snapper," a personal catchphrase that captures the message of the dream and orients you toward forward movement.
- Go back inside the dream through the dream reentry technique (see chapter 5).
- Research names, locales, and other significant details from the dream.
- Keep the dream in mind as a travel advisory or a rehearsal for future developments.
- Share the dream with someone else who may need its guidance.
- Write/paint/create to honor the dream.
- Make a dream talisman.

Walking a Dream

Janice likes to walk dreams as you or I might walk the dog. Sometimes she walks her own dreams. As a very active member of an online dream-sharing community I founded, she often walks other people's dreams, like one of those professional dog walkers you see with half a dozen canines of all sizes on a fistful of leashes. As she strolls around, she finds that fresh insights come to her easily and naturally. Sometimes an incident gives her a second opinion on a dream. This might be the sigh of the wind in the trees, or the flight of a bird, or a snatch of overheard conversation.

I love this approach, which has something in common with Jung's preferred mode of "circumambulation" in approaching the meaning of a dream. Jung felt he came closer to the heart of a dream when he wandered around it, looking at it from different angles, rather than trying to mount a direct assault on its inner keep.

So walking a dream can be just what the phrase suggests. Janice — a shrewd and stylish New Yorker who worked in sales for many years and is now a teacher of Active Dreaming — adds a further twist to her dream walking. "I like to wear my dreams the day after," she says. This might mean dressing in the style or dominant color of a dream or carrying accessories that evoke something of the dream.

Let's review some other options for walking our dreams.

One of the most ancient is to create or obtain an object that can serve as a dream amulet by holding and focusing the energy and guidance of a powerful dream. In a healing retreat for women vets, six participants worked together on a dream of a red dress. When the dreamer was able to see herself wearing that red dress and going boldly through a gateway that had been closed to her in the original dream, a profound energy shift took place and deep healing became available to all of the women in the group. While the dreamer's action plans naturally included "wearing the dream" by getting a red dress, the six women agreed they wanted to make dream amulets that would keep them connected and keep the wonderful energy they had developed working for all of them. To accomplish this, they chose special beads, which they attached to ribbons the same color as the dream dress and fastened to their key rings.

I like key-ring amulets. Every time you take out your keys to enter your house or car, you are reminded of your dream, and you may find it is one of the most important keys on the chain. Some dreamers who have worked with me inscribe a catchphrase or "banner" from a dream on a tag and put that on their key ring. "It's all about me" was the dream tag of a woman going through a difficult divorce after a dream instructed her that it was time to stop being a team player and insist on her own needs. Not original, but right for that particular life passage. And she can change the phrase when life, and her dreams, give her a fresh message.

Research is often an action required by a dream. Dreams can prompt us to do detailed research on content, ranging from an obscure word to the natural habits of an animal that appeared or a way to fix a fuse box. This can go far beyond simply clarifying the initial information. Dream clues can put us on the trail of very important discoveries, ranging from our connection to a spiritual tradition that is calling us, to a new book idea, to what's going on behind closed doors in Washington.

When you dream of a certain animal, you'll want to research its natural habits and habitat to understand its relevance to you and the way you relate to the natural path of your energies. This means doing something better than just consulting some guide to animal totems; it means studying the animal in the way of a naturalist, in nature if possible — perhaps on the way to feeding and nourishing it in your body and in the way you use that body.

That strange name you dreamed, or phrase in a language you don't know, or know imperfectly, can be a clue to a world of knowledge that was previously closed to you. My life has been changed and my horizon of understanding expanded enormously by odd words left over from night dreams that have led me on long trails of research and exploration. Words like *ondinnonk*, for example, which sounded like nonsense until I discovered that, in archaic Huron-Mohawk, it means "the secret wish of the soul," especially as revealed in dreams. Sometimes it has taken me years, or an improbable chain of chance events, to crack such codes, but in the age of the Internet, dream-directed research can speed along much faster than in the past.

Jung said that his dreams spurred all his important study. He observed in *Memories, Dreams, Reflections*: "All day long I have exciting ideas and thoughts. But I take up in my work only those to which my dreams direct me." My own studies are similarly guided, but I would expand the word *dreams* to include waking experiences of meaningful coincidence when we feel we are receiving a secret handshake or a nudge or a wink from the universe.

The action a dream requires may be to carry and apply its navigational guidance. It's my impression that the dream self is forever traveling ahead of the waking self, scouting the roads we have not yet taken. By studying closely where our dream self has traveled into the possible future, we can decide whether we want to follow in its tracks or take a different way. We may see a future event we cannot change but can handle better — and help others to handle better — because we remember and apply what showed up on our dream radar.

Here's a moving example. Carol dreamed that her nephew told her that Cody, the beloved family dog, had died. In her dream, she then saw Cody as a bounding, frisky puppy, running around in a happy scene. In waking reality, Cody was elderly but still alive. Carol took the dream as an alert to be ready to support her brother's family in the event of Cody's death. She was with the family on the day Cody died. She was then able to tell them, "You know, Cody is still with you." When she recounted her dream of seeing Cody in his new life as a bounding puppy, a sense of blessing and joy replaced the feelings of grief in the family. Soon Carol's relatives were laughing as they shared reminiscences of Cody, including the day when he had nearly choked on a pecan pie.

Many dreams invite us to create from them and with them, through our favorite media and also through media with which we may be less familiar or less confident. Write, sculpt, draw, dance, paint, or move with the dream, and if you have friends or family who'll play, turn it into performance or theater. Some dreams want to explode into paint on canvas. Others flow effortlessly into poetry. Some make us pick up our feet and move or dance. Some get us down on the floor with crayons or cutting up old magazines with scissors for a collage. Some dreams want to be baked or stirred.

Writing the Next Chapter

You can write the next chapter of a dream (or a life passage).

In a series of dreams, Jenny was attacked again and again by a horrible, scary black bug that was trying to invade her body. A gentle student of Buddhism, Jenny tried a gentle response. In dream reentry, she tried to dialogue with the bug. This bug was not in a talking mood. In a creepy, conscious dream experience, the bug tried to rip a hole in her torso to get inside.

When Jenny shared this, I suggested that if this were my dream, I would stop trying to converse with the bug, give up on further attempts at dream reentry, and instead *write* the "next chapter," in which I would try to resolve everything in whatever way felt right.

Jenny accepted this assignment. She wrote a scene in which she cast the bug and the illness it represented out of her body and her life. When she read to an active dream circle the passionate, searing words she composed, we all saw and felt a tremendous positive shift in her energy and knew that she had just taken a huge step in healing.

What we can always do with a dream is enter it in our secret book.

4

Keeping Your Books of Night and Day

I am enamored of my journal.

— SIR WALTER SCOTT

When a lusty, ambitious young Scot named James Boswell first met Dr. Samuel Johnson, Johnson advised him to keep a journal of his life. Boswell responded that he was already journaling, recording "all sorts of little incidents." Dr. Johnson said, "Sir, there is nothing too little for so little a creature as man."

Indeed, there is nothing too little, or too great, for inclusion in a journal. If you are not already keeping one, please start *today*. Write whatever is passing through your mind, or whatever catches your eye in the passing scene around you. If you remember your dreams, start with them. If you don't recall your dreams, start with whatever thoughts and feelings are first with you as you enter the day.

If you have any hopes of becoming a writer, you'll find that journaling is your daily workout that keeps your writing muscles limber. If you are already a writer, you may find that as you set things down just as they come, with no concern for editors, critics, or consequences, you are releasing descriptive scenes, narrative solutions, characters — even entire first drafts — effortlessly.

Some of the most productive writers have also been prodigious journal keepers. Graham Greene started recording dreams when he was sixteen, after a breakdown in school. His journals from the last quarter century of his life survive in the all-but-unbreakable code of his difficult handwriting. First and last, he recorded his dreams, and — as I describe in detail in my *Secret History of Dreaming* — they gave him plot solutions, character development, insights into the nature of reality that he attributed to some of his characters, and sometimes bridge scenes that could be troweled directly into a narrative. Best of all, journaling *kept him going*, enabling him to crank out his daily pages for publication no matter how many gins or how much cloak-and-dagger activity or illicit amour he had indulged in the night before.

You don't have to be a writer to be a journaler, but journal keeping will make you a writer anyway. In the pages of your journal, you will meet yourself in all your aspects. As you keep a journal over the years, you'll notice the rhymes and loops or cycles in your life. Mircea Eliade, the great Romanian-born historian of religions, was a great journaler. In the last volume of his published journals, he reflects, during a visit to Amsterdam in 1974, on how a bitter setback to his hopes at the time he first visited that city, nearly a quarter century before, had driven him to do his most enduring work. He had been hoping during his earlier visit that his early autobiographical novel, published in English as *Bengal Nights*, would be a big commercial success, enabling him to live as a full-time novelist. Sales had been disappointing. Had it been otherwise, "I would have devoted almost all my time to literature and relegated the history of religions to second place, even though *Shamanism* was at the time almost entirely drafted."[7] The world would have gained a promising, and perhaps eventually first-class, novelist; but we might have lost the scholar who first made the study of shamanism academically respectable and proceeded to breathe vibrant life into the cross-cultural study of the human interaction with the sacred.

Synesius of Cyrene, a heterodox bishop in North Africa around 400, counseled in a wonderful essay, "On Dreams," that we should keep twin journals: a journal of the night and a journal of the day. In the night journal, we would record dreams as the products of a "personal oracle" and a direct line to the God we can talk to. In the day journal, we would track the signs and correspondences through which the world around us is constantly speaking in a symbolic code. "All things are signs appearing through all things. They are brothers in a single living creature, the cosmos." The sage is one who "understands the relationship of the parts of the universe"[8] — and we deepen and focus that understanding by recording signs in our day journal.

Partly because I keep unusual hours and am often embarked on my best creative work long before dawn, I don't separate my night journal from my day journal. All the material goes into one book of changing heft and composition — a leather-bound travel journal when I am on the road, a big three-ring binder at home. I try to type up my entries before my handwriting (as difficult as Greene's) becomes illegible and put the printouts in binders. I save each entry with a date and a title in my data files, so I automatically have a running index.

Six Games to Play with Your Secret Book

When you write in your journal, you are keeping a date with your Self. I'm giving "self" a big *S* because I'm talking about something bigger than the everyday mind, so often prone to distraction or mixed-up agendas, so driven by routines and other people's requirements.

A date with the Self should be *fun*. Here are six everyday games to play with your journal.

Write Your Way Through

Whatever ails you or bugs you or blocks you, write about it. Getting it out is immediate therapy. If you keep your journal strictly private (which is essential, by the way), what you put down in these pages can be your everyday confessional, with the cleansing and release that can bring. It's funny how, when you start by recording your woes, something else comes into play that brings you up instead of down and can actually restore your sense of humor.

When you see and state things as they are, you already begin to change them. Keep your hand moving, and you may manifest the power to rename and re-vision symptoms, challenges, and difficult situations in the direction of resolution and healing.

Catch Your Dreams

Every time you remember a dream, record it. Date your entry and give the dream a title. By giving a name to a dream, you are recognizing that there's a story to be told, and that you are now in the process of becoming a storyteller. Also jot down your feelings about the dream; your first feelings on waking are the best guidance on what it is telling you.

Make a Book of Clues

The world is speaking to us through coincidence and chance encounters and symbolic pop-ups, giving us clues to the hidden logic of events. Once we start paying attention, we find that synchronicity is a fabulous source of navigational guidance. Write down in your journal anything unusual or unexpected that you notice during the day. Suggestion: note in your journal what appears on the first vanity license plate you spot each day.

Collect Pick-Me-Up Lines

No, I did *not* say "pick-up lines"! One of the things I treasure in my own journals, and in those of famous dead people that I read, is the collection of interesting and inspiring quotes that grows once we get into the habit of jotting down one-liners that catch our attention. Some recent examples from my own journaling:

"Because we are stars, we must walk the sky." — Song of Bushmen
    lion shamans
"An idea is salvation by imagination." — Frank Lloyd Wright
"You have other centuries to play with." — Seth, in Jane Roberts's
    The Nature of Personal Reality
"Something always goes wrong or there wouldn't be a story."
    — Charles de Lint
"Coincidences are spiritual puns." — G.K. Chesterton
EZ GOES — vanity plate on a car in front of me

Make Your Own Dictionary of Symbols

Tracking how symbols feature and evolve in your dreams and your experience of the world around you will give you your own encyclopedia of symbols, far superior to all those dream dictionaries, because the snake or the train in your dream is *yours*, not theirs.

The images that arise in our dreams and in the play of coincidence in waking life often seem to link us to the realm of the archetypes, to universal symbols that seem to repeat again and again in the collective mind of humanity. At the same time, the images that arise spontaneously in dreaming are individual, our personal gifts, and we don't want to assign an external authority the responsibility of determining the meaning of our dreams or our lives.

It's fascinating to watch how a personal symbol can evolve over time. Thus the wild animal that scared you in one dream may become your ally when you brave up in a later dream. Or what seemed to be your childhood home turns out to have many more levels than you remember, opening a sense of expanding life possibilities. Again, we study this by journaling and linking our reports on a recurring theme.

I keep a thematic index of my dream reports that is very close to a personal encyclopedia of symbols. Animals figure prominently: Fox and Bear, Black Dog and White Wolf. So do recurring locales and modes of transportation: Houses and Theaters, Trains and Planes.

Living symbols take us beyond what we ordinarily know, and are never still but constantly evolving.

Write Until You're a Writer

Sit down with your journal every day and keep your hand moving, and before you think about it you'll find you have become a writer. Whether the world knows that, or whether you choose to share your writing with the world, is secondary. You are writing for your Self, and without fear of the consequences. You are giving your writing muscles a workout, and you'll find it tones up your whole system.

Writer and creativity coach Robin O'Neal Kissel shares this account of what keeping a dream journal has meant for her:

I have found the practice of journaling my dreams has significantly impacted the way in which I write about waking reality. As I write a night dream as a story, it calls on me to take my waking writer's mind back into the world of the dream on a quest to capture the imagery, the emotion, the sequence... the very texture of the dream experience. In writing a dream narrative, I strive to honor fully the depth of the experience of my dream, owning it and making it real with words.

I have gained much as a *dreamer* via this process, because that which is honored and owned multiplies and expands, blooming in the nurturing, thriving with attention. I have also gained much as a *writer*. I approach the act of journaling my daily events as if they, too, are a dream — the dream that happens on this side of my consciousness. I explore the events of my waking life with an eye to capturing the imagery, emotion, sequence, and texture, telling it as a story, seeking to comprehend symbolism and synchronicity, just as I would a dream. In both instances, I take myself back into the scene unfolding and narrate in the present tense — the act of writing in present tense requires that I be fully present to the story unfolding. Often, recounting the experience this way is tantamount to "reentry," and I'm astounded by the new comprehension or creative stirrings of forward momentum that transpire within, and because of, the process itself.

Six Deeper Games to Play with Your Secret Book

Journaling is a practice, and as in any true practice, you have to earn the right of admission to the more advanced levels. Here are six deeper games to play with your journal when you've been journaling for at least one year.

Bibliomancy

Bibliomancy is the fancy name for opening a book at random to get guidance on a theme or simply a guide to the quality and content of the day. In Western countries, over the centuries the Bible has been the hands-down favorite for use as a book oracle. Abraham Lincoln used to open his family Bible — the one on which Barack Obama took his oath of office — to get a message for the day or a second opinion on the meaning of a dream.

I enjoy doing bibliomancy with my old journals. One Christmas Eve, after learning that a friend had developed a serious illness and was having other major troubles in her life, I reached blindly into a shelf of more than thirty old travel journals, grabbed one without looking at the date, and opened it at random. I found myself looking at a short dream report from five years earlier. The dream was about my friend. It stated that she had "accepted purgatory for a year. This purgatory is a room in her home that opens into the same realm." I shared this report with my friend, and we began to work with the meaning of *acceptance* and of *purgatory*. Our mutual exploration provided assurance that "this too shall pass," and that a year in "purgatory" would result in healing and new growth, as proved to be the case.

Compare Your Dream Self to Your Waking Self

Are you running away from something in your dreams? Ask yourself when you tend to run away from something — a person, an issue, a necessary conversation — in regular life.

Does your dream self have supernormal powers? Can she fly or knock villains down like ninepins? If so, then ask yourself where you might be able to draw on her courage and powers in the rest of your life.

Comparing the behavior of the dream self and that of the waking self is highly instructive. We may also find that bringing gifts and qualities from one realm into the other can be tremendously healing and empowering. My waking self may be able to bring courage — the determination to brave up to a challenge — to a dream self that is frightened or frozen.

My dream self who is fluent in another language, or can breathe underwater, may be able to give me the power to expand my vocabulary of understanding or to operate with ease in a new environment.

Dialogue with Your Other Selves

Sit down with your journal and imagine yourself talking to a character from one of your dreams. Since everything is alive in dreams, you can ask anything from a dream — a horse, a house, an eighteen-wheeler —

to talk to you. You can call up every character and element from a dream and ask them to explain themselves in turn, if you like.

Start out with a question like "Who are you?" or "What are you doing in my dream?"

Move on to a question like "What can you tell me?"

Be ready to be surprised! You may find you are interviewing sides of yourself you never knew were part of your family of personality aspects. You may find you are talking to a departed loved one, or an ancestor, or the guy who owned the house fifty years ago. You may even encounter a dream character who tells you: "I am dreaming you. You are in my dream."

Reopen Your Cold Case Files

Dreams give us clues that require sleuthing, but sometimes our best attempts to follow these leads don't get far and we move on to other things, leaving a mounting pile of "cold case" files. I pick up a lot of unfamiliar names, foreign words, and curious phrases in dreams and — especially — in the twilight state of hypnagogia, and I have found it extraordinarily revealing to track these verbal clues. In the era of Googling, this is much easier than it was over most of the decades I've been keeping a journal, so I am now reopening dream files I had closed and making some exciting discoveries. One of those funny words, from a 1994 dream, led me to an archaeological site in Nigeria where the human remains date from 10,000 BCE. Another is guiding me, in the most practical way, on professional decisions I'll be making over the next couple of months.

Be open to discovering that an event in an "old" dream is starting to manifest only now — months or years later — and be ready (beyond the "wow" response) to harvest guidance from the old report on the current situation. When you see a match-up between an "old" dream and a later event, forage around the individual report: look at other dreams from about the same time and see if there are further clues to the new situation.

Let Out the Artist inside You

I often type my journal reports directly into a computer to save the time required for transcription from a manuscript version and to get around the problem of finding it hard to decipher my own handwriting. When I write by hand, however, I find there's an artist in me who wants to come bursting through. Suddenly the pages facing my text reports are filled with drawings that may then demand to be colored in or painted. Some of these drawings occupy successive panels like pages from a graphic novel. The famous movie director Federico Fellini, who started out as a cartoonist, kept dream journals that are primarily visual.

Many dream journalers find they have a poet inside. Or a song-writer. Sometimes a whole poem or song is delivered within a dream or in that fluid in-between zone of sleep-wake, *dorveille*. Some dream re-ports, with a little editing, effortlessly turn into poems. Every dream contains a story; some want to be stories in the fuller and finished sense, and journaling will get you there.

Journal from Journals

Thoreau journaled all the time. He wrote down his observations of na-ture, his thoughts and dreams, his notes on his constant reading. Most interesting, he journaled from his journals, picking over old volumes, plucking out promising bits and pieces, copying them out and marrying them up to make fresh drafts. It became his habit to revisit old journals, revise old materials, and weave together different passages.

I can't recommend this practice too highly. For any writer, as for Thoreau, it opens treasuries of material, and above all, it supports the writing *habit*. Playing around with old notes removes the terror of the blank page. When you dip into an old journal, you are never at a loss for a theme. The simple processes of selection, arrangement, and retitling will fire the imagination. Before you know it, you'll be in the midst of writing something new.

As you tend your secret book over time, you'll discover more, and more will discover you. There are even deeper games you'll be able to play. You'll find yourself straying out of the tame and settled territory of the everyday mind and into the wilder borders of imagination, where the big story of your life can find you.

5

Shamanic Lucid Dreaming

*Shamanic activity...makes use of the ordinary
(that which is available to all) in extraordinary ways.*

—— ANGELA SUMEGI,
Dreamworlds of Shamanism and Tibetan Buddhism

I'm not very keen about the term *lucid dreaming*, because it has often been associated with the preposterous notion of "controlling" dreams. For the ego to set out to control the dreamworld is as silly as Canute trying to stop the waves of the sea. The ocean of dreaming is infinitely deeper and wiser than the daily trivial mind. Our enterprise should be to navigate its waters, not control them.

Then again, the term *lucid dreaming* is often associated with techniques for waking yourself up to the fact that you are dreaming while you are asleep. Such techniques range from using goggles with flashing lights to self-programming to check whether you are dreaming every time you look at your hands or in a mirror. But the easiest way to become a lucid, or *conscious*, dreamer is to start out lucid and stay that way: in other words, to enter conscious dreaming from a waking or semiwakeful state.

I must add that the Dutchman who coined the term *lucid dreaming*, Frederik van Eeden, was awash with bizarre notions about sexuality and demons; those who borrow from his famous paper on the subject would do well to study his strange, autobiographical novel, *The Bride of Dreams*, as well.[9]

But the discussion of lucid dreaming has matured in recent years, especially with the publication of Robert Waggoner's excellent book *Lucid Dreaming: Gateway to the Inner Self*. And since I am often asked whether Active Dreaming is a mode of lucid dreaming, I am going to borrow a phrase employed by one of my friends in the lucid-dreaming fraternity, who refers to my "shamanic lucid dream adventures." The word *shamanic* is also problematic, of course, since the word *shaman* is used in so many ways. I am using the adjective here to describe a method for shifting consciousness in order to enter nonordinary reality for purposes that include the care and recovery of *soul*. In this chapter, we'll explore how Active Dreaming goes beyond most approaches to lucid dreaming. In the next, we'll learn how the core techniques of Active Dreaming can be used to facilitate adventures in shared dreaming with one or more partners.

Taking Off in the Twilight Zone

Once more, with feeling: the easiest way to become a *conscious* dream traveler is to start out conscious and stay that way. How do you do that? Really, you only need three things: a clear intention, an image that can serve as a portal, and a means of focusing the mind and fueling the journey.

All these things can become available naturally and effortlessly in the twilight zone of consciousness that researchers call hypnagogia. In it, you are between sleep and waking. Images rise and fall in your mind, if you let them, and any one of those images can become the gateway for a conscious dream adventure. In this liminal state, we also make creative connections that escape the ordinary mind. In my *Secret History of Dreaming*, I call this the "solution state" because it has been the field for breakthrough discoveries in the history of science as well as many other fields.

When you develop the ability to enter and remain in a state of relaxed, free-flowing awareness, images will come. You can simply observe them as they rise and fall, or engage with one of these images or scenes and enter into what may be a full-fledged dream journey.

The term *twilight zone* evokes the brilliant old TV series by that name and (for me) the no less clever contemporary series of fantasy novels by the Russian author Sergei Lukyanenko. In Lukyanenko's *Night Watch* and its sequels, *Twilight* is the term used for levels of reality beyond the physical plane. Rival magicians develop the power to see into — and travel through — deepening levels of Twilight by "pulling up" their shadows and stepping through them. (Sadly, in the movie version no effort is made to depict this; the characters just put on dark glasses like Neo and Morpheus in *The Matrix*.)

When you let yourself slip into the twilight zone, you may have the impression that someone is waiting for you or has something to tell you. Visitations are common in the liminal state, on the cusp of sleep. You may find yourself looking at a sea of faces, scanning or simply drifting through the psychic environment around you. You may pick up some of the human noise band, hearing voices and bursts of radio-like transmissions blurring into static.

You may see unusual colors and textures. In many of my own twilight experiences, I find myself drawn into richly textured fabric patterns. I used to think of these as my "Persian rug" or "magic carpet" experiences. The magic carpet effect was different than in the fairy tales, but no less magical. I would find myself looking more and more closely at the threads of the fabric. Proportions and perspective would shift until I could slip between the threads and pop out in a different scene — and take off into conscious dream adventures.

As you begin to surface from sleep, you may find you are still strongly connected with the energy and imagery of sleep dreams. If you can allow yourself some undisturbed time in bed, you may be able to slip back into the dreamspace, fully conscious, or allow new dreams to unfold as you remain conscious.

Here are a few travel reports of conscious dream adventures that begin in the twilight zone, starting with one of my own.

From Running to Flying

Lying on my back in bed, awake and ready for the gates of perception to open into another world, I find myself running, faster and faster, over open country. This is a highly kinesthetic experience that fully engages my inner senses. My heartbeat quickens, my legs fly across the grass. Soon I am bounding over hills and valleys, springing over the landscape like a kangaroo.

Effortlessly, without thinking about it, I become airborne. For a time, I am speeding along just a few feet above the ground, following its contours. As I continue to gain speed, I gain altitude. Soon I am looking down at the winding course of a stream from hundreds of feet up.

I realize I need to establish a flight plan, or I might fall and be grounded. I decide to drop in on a friend. I've never been to her home, but when I think of her, I am instantly there, in a modest house with washing on a line in the yard. I take her flying high above the earth.

When I share my impressions the next day, this friend confirms my description of her house and says she has just hung washing on the line. She also recalls a dream in which we flew together to a city in the sky.

Off into the Starry Night

Michele reports:

I lie down and close my eyes. It is dark and there are swirls of mist and fog. It parts somewhat to unveil the starry sky. It is a sky like I've never seen before, with completely foreign constellations. I seek to find Orion or Cassiopeia, without luck, and am drawn deeper and deeper into a deep, expansive meditative state.

The misty swirls remain as I excitedly lie and watch the stars above as if I am lying in an open field and simply looking at the stars. Other images come and go, but I love this one and decide I want to go back to it. I find myself in the same spot as before, and I gratefully sink into the bliss of the deep starry night.

Parade of Faces

Seeing a parade of faces is a common experience in the twilight zone, as in the following report:

> Usually, I see distinct faces of various people from varied cultural backgrounds, from different eras — dressed in detail. Sometimes they are doing something, and sometimes they just pop in. I love this part of sleeping. I am thrilled to remember each face and hairdo and detail of clothing. I ask myself why are they appearing to me. There have been times when they have tried to speak. Their mouths move, but the sounds coming from their mouths are not in sync, like when the lips of actors on TV are moving but the words don't match.

Dream House with Wave Panther

Janice started out designing a home at the beach and got something unexpected:

> One night, in the twilight zone, I amuse myself by designing a house for myself. My mind goes to a beach house on the oceanfront at night. The moon is full and casts its shadow like a glistening white runway along the dark water. There are burning lamps on the sand running up to the house, in a parallel formation, with lots of sand in between.
>
> Then a huge ocean wave rolls in. As it crests, a panther's head breaks through, followed by its body. The panther is gracefully deposited right on the beach as the wave rolls in to shore. The sea panther, born from the waves, is totally unexpected, and thrilling. Later, in dreams and journeys I am able to claim the panther as an animal guardian.

Incubating a Conscious Dream

Just as we can set an intention for our sleep dreams, we can incubate a conscious dream experience. On a night when I felt in need of some personal healing, I did this in the way of the ancient pilgrims who journeyed to the temples of Asklepios.

Sitting up in bed, I stated my intention in clear and simple language: *I wish to be healed.* Mindful that, in seeking gifts from a higher power, it is always a good idea to ask nicely, I added this statement: *I ask for the health of body and mind required to serve my spiritual purpose.*

Here's my raw journal report on what ensued:

A Night of Asklepian Dream Healing

I stretch out on the bed. Immediately, I see an enormous serpent. It is gray-blue and could be twenty feet long. I see the dark slits of its pupils, close to me, in a head larger than my own. I do not feel fear, but there is a strong sense of the uncanny, the presence of a transpersonal other. I feel this is the Asklepian serpent, a power mastered for healing.

I resolve to let the snake enter my energy field and do anything required for healing. I begin to experience the movement of the serpent energy through my chakras, starting at the root center and traveling upward. There are moments of gentle physical pressure or constriction as it passes through some of my energy centers — of slight pressure in the heart, of a little constriction at the throat. The movement ceases to flow smoothly at the vision center, where I had been experiencing pressure and blurring. An experimental probe, not pushing too hard. The movement loops down and back, returning to try again.

I invoke light as well and feel the presence and blessing of a being of light I know well. I feel a process of healing has been initiated and will be played out over time if I allow it to be.

All of this has been enacted in the liminal state of wake-dream, which is where much of the work of Asklepian healing took place. Now I let myself drift toward sleep, hoping for the gift of further healing in the dreamspace. That gift comes in the form of an amazing and energizing sleep dream that connects my personal healing to new creative endeavors, writing new books and bringing them to the world.

Dream Reentry

An equally simple and natural way to become a conscious dreamer is to use a remembered dream as the portal for a journey. Think of it this way: in your night dream, you went to a place that may resemble a site in ordinary reality, or that may be somewhere extraordinary where the physics are utterly different. Either way, because you were in a certain place, you may be able to find your way back there, just as you could return to a café or bookshop or house party you once visited in your regular life.

Why would you want to do such a thing? There are plenty of excellent reasons. Maybe you've been running away from your dreams, and leaving them broken and unfinished, because there's something in your dream world that scares you. If you can find the courage to go back inside one of those nightmares, wide awake and conscious, and face what frightened you, it's more than likely you'll find power and healing waiting for you on the other side of the terror. The fiercest dragons guard the richest treasures, said Rilke with a poet's clarity.

You may want to go back inside a dream because you were having a great time that was interrupted by the alarm clock or the kids tickling your toes. You may want to go back in to have more of a conversation with someone who appeared to you in a dream — your departed grandmother, maybe, or a wise old man you suspect is a guide — or to read a letter you left unread. You may want to see what's on the top floor of that mysterious house, or down in the root cellar. You may have a mystery to solve. You may want to clarify whether that plane crash could take place in the future, as either a literal or symbolic event, and what you need to do with that information (once it's clear) in order to avoid or contain an unwanted development. You may simply want to know more about a dream. The best way to understand a dream is to recover more of the experience of the dream. Dreams are experiences, not texts, and a dream experience fully remembered is its own interpretation.

Through the technique of dream reentry, you can pursue any of these agendas or simply enjoy the fun and adventure of using a personal dream image as a portal to the multiverse. The best time to attempt dream reentry may be when the dream is fresh and you are still closely connected to it — while lazing in bed after waking, or slipping back into bed after a bathroom stop. But if the dream has energy for you, you may be able to go back inside it long afterward.

A woman in one of my workshops told us she had not remembered *any* dreams for all of thirty years but had come to us with a keen interest in revisiting the last dream she remembered, from when she was a teenager. We created a space in which she was able to reenter that dream, which had a huge emotional charge because it had come on the night of her father's death. The preliminary to her dream reentry journey was to call back the original dream and get it clear in her mind and in her senses, and to state a clear and simple intention, which included the desire to reconnect with her father. In that workshop circle, we used shamanic drumming to focus and power the journey. The woman who had not remembered a dream in thirty years succeeded brilliantly in getting back inside this one, assisted by the drumming and by the supportive energy of the circle. She succeeded in meeting her father, and we were deeply moved by her account of the love and forgiveness they were able to exchange. When the drum sounded the end of the conscious dream journey, she told us that she glimpsed dozens of the dreams she had lost over thirty years, fluttering about her like glorious butterflies. Some of those lost dreams returned with her, and with them came the shimmering energy of soul.

For ancient and indigenous shamans, the chief cause of many of our complaints — fatigue, low energy, excessive vulnerability to illness and allergies — is soul loss. The understanding is that, in any human life, we may lose part of our vital energy and identity through pain or grief, shame or abuse, or wrenching life choices. The cure is to find that missing piece and bring it back and put it where it belongs.

For me, soul recovery is central to healing. In order to be whole and able to operate with the best and brightest parts of our beings, we may need to recover parts of ourselves that have gone missing. While we can look to a shamanic practitioner — if we can find a reliable and responsible one — to assist us through the operation known as soul retrieval, it may be safer and more empowering to learn the techniques that will enable us to be self-healers and shamans for our own family of selves.

Our dreams offer us roads to soul recovery. You dream of being back in the old place. This may be your childhood home or the place you shared with your ex. Such dreams may be telling you that you left a part of yourself at that place at a certain time in your life. They may be issuing an invitation for you to reach back into that time and place and reclaim something that belongs to you — that beautiful younger person whose dreams were interrupted but can now be lived by you, if you are reunited.

Maybe you've been dreaming of a younger person of the same gender as yourself who may turn out to be your own younger self. (Sometimes it takes a while to recognize just who that dream character is.) This is an even stronger invitation to soul integration: to reach out to that younger self and bring his or her energy into your heart and your body.

Your dreams about shoes (shoes have "soles") may be another clue to the condition and location of aspects of your soul.

Soul recovery, in the fullest sense, is not only about reclaiming our younger selves. It is also about meeting and integrating all our personality aspects, including as much of the energy and insight of the larger or higher Self as we can manage to contain at this stage in our life journey.

EXERCISE

Dream Reentry Adventures

You prepare to reenter a dream as follows:

1. *Pick a dream that has some real energy for you.* It doesn't matter whether it is a dream from last night or from twenty years ago, as long as it has juice. It doesn't matter whether it is a tiny fragment or a complex narrative. It makes no difference whether you choose to work with a night dream, a vision, or a waking image. What's important is that the dream you choose to revisit has some juice — whether it is exciting, seductive, or challenging.

2. *Begin to relax.* Follow the flow of your breathing. If you are holding tension in any part of your body, tense and relax the muscle groups associated with that part of your body until you feel yourself becoming loose and comfy in your body.

3. *Focus on a specific scene from your dream.* Let it become vivid on your mental screen. See if you can let all your senses become engaged, so you can touch it, smell it, hear it, taste it.

4. *Clarify your intention.* Come up with clear and simple answers to these two questions:

    -   What do you want to *know*?
    -   What do you intend to *do* once you are back inside the dream?

You may need one thing more: something to energize your adventure in conscious dreaming and to help you shut out distracting thoughts. Shamanic drumming — a steady beat on a simple frame drum, typically in the range of four beats per second (but sometimes faster) — is a marvelous tool for helping to shift consciousness and travel into the dreamspace. The steady beats serve to override mental clutter and focus energy and intention on the journey. The rhythms of the drum correspond to brain-wave frequencies in the theta band, associated with the hypnagogic zone and its dreamlike imagery. If you want a physiological explanation of why shamanic drumming is such a powerful tool for shifting awareness, you could say that the "sonic driving" of the drum herds our brain waves into the theta band, opening us to its characteristic flow of imagery.

For whatever reason, steady drumming often facilitates, accelerates, deepens, and synchronizes the experience of conscious dreaming in a workshop setting. You may want to experiment with my CD of shamanic drumming for dream travelers, *Wings for the Journey* (see the "Resources" section at the back of the present book).

When you reenter a dream, you can invite one or more friends to go with you to support you as you face your dream challenges on their own ground, and to gather information for your benefit. When two or more people are able to enter the same space in nonordinary reality and bring back mutually confirming information from that space, they have produced hard evidence of the objective reality of other realms. Through

this process, we can bring back immensely valuable guidance and healing help for each other. This is one of the modes of shared dreaming
we'll explore in the next chapter.

Dreaming with the Animal Powers

When shamans go dreaming, characteristically they operate under the
protection and guidance of animal guardians. Forging a close relationship with one or more "power animals" is central to developing the arts
of shamanic dream travel and tracking. It is invaluable in maintaining
healthy boundaries and defending psychic space. A conscious connection with the animal guardians shows us how to follow the natural paths
of our energy. A strong working connection with the animal powers
gives us the ability to shape-shift the energy body and project energy
forms that can operate at a distance from the physical body.

Our ancestors believed that we are born with a connection to a particular totem animal; this was the raison d'être of the clan system. Some
Australian Aborigines believe even today that, when a human is born, its
"bush soul" is born in the form of an animal or bird. We may feel that
we have a lifelong connection with a certain animal or bird. Others may
observe this in our body type, our lifestyles, our modes of responding to
challenges.

But in the course of a lifetime, we may develop many animal connections. Some of these may stem from our relations with the animals
who share our homes and habitats, ranging from the family pets to wild
animals encountered in nature and in our travels. Animals we have met
in the physical world may reappear in our dreams as allies and helpers.

Animal dreams may be the doorway to developing strong working
relations with the animal guardians. These dreams may hold up a mirror
that reflects our health or habits. They may show us how we need to feed
and attend to our bodies. They may reveal a potential we have not yet
developed. They may tell a story about our lives or relationships like one
of Aesop's fables. They may be the place of encounter between our dream

self and a spiritual ally or guardian. Our true spiritual teachers come looking for us in our dreams, and often they come in unexpected forms.

Active dreamers develop strong connections with their animal guardians. These are *energy* connections, not simply objects of personal symbolism. Active dreamers learn to borrow the senses and skills of the animal powers in order to track, to establish well-controlled psychic boundaries, and to heal. One of the fastest ways I know to restore vitality, to restore the immune system, and to move beyond lethargy or depression is to connect with the animal spirits.

I provide detailed guidance to connecting and working with the animal powers in my previous books, especially *Conscious Dreaming*, *Dreamgates*, and *Dreamways of the Iroquois*, and I will not revisit that material here. In chapter 9, "Mapping the Natural Path of Your Energy," I offer a fresh approach that will help you identify and recruit your animal spirits.

6

Social and Shared Dreaming

In Aboriginal Australia . . . dreams can be a shared experience. In the Wirrimanu area, it was not uncommon for two individuals to say they had shared the same dream. . . . There were also instances when, as other dreamers dreamed, they decided to enter yet another person's dream or were attracted to the action occurring in a dream setting.

— SYLVIE POIRIER, "This Is Good Country. We Are Good Dreamers"

Conscious dream travel is an adventure we can share with a partner, with a group, or with a whole community. While we tend to think of dreams as private and personal, dreaming is actually a highly social activity. Many of us, indeed, are far more gregarious in our dreams than in our ordinary daily lives. As we share dreams with friends and family on a regular basis, we may notice that sometimes our dreams overlap closely. A husband and wife I know dreamed on the same night that they had a date at a Victoria's Secret store — inside a church!

We may dream on the same theme, or visit the same dreamscape, on the same night. Sometimes we have shared adventures, though (more often than not) only one of the dreamers remembers exactly what was going on.

We are drawn together in dreams in the same ways that we are drawn to each other in waking life: by family ties, by shared interests, by common concerns, by love and sexual attraction, by the need for healing or the desire for fun and adventure. As we become active dreamers, we can develop the practice of embarking on conscious interactive dream journeys with focused intention. We can do this up close or at any distance. We can learn to enter shared dreaming with an intimate partner who shares our bed, with a group of friends in a living room, or with a network of dreamers in other parts of the world.

Let's pause to define the varieties of social dreaming:

Synchronous or concurrent dreams are those in which two or more dreamers have very similar dream experiences at the same time. They may or may not see each other inside the dreams.

Interactive or mutual dreams are those in which two or more dreamers are aware of each other and interact with each other in a shared dreamscape. In terms of ordinary time, their experiences may or may not be synchronous.

Shared dreaming, in my lexicon, is the practice of embarking on intentional interactive dream travels with one or more partners.

Group dreaming, or group dream travel, is shared dreaming conducted with a whole circle or network of participants.

Shared Dreaming as Home Entertainment

You're separated from your sweetheart and you'd like to have some good private time together. Can you do that? Absolutely. As the old song says, "You can reach [him or her] with your mind." The next question is: your place or mine, or somewhere else altogether? How about meeting up at an elegant restaurant in Paris, or on a lava beach in Hawaii, or at the Moon Café (in the astral realm of Luna, don't you know?), where the bubbly is better than any earthly brand of champagne. *You can do this.*

If you are embarking on shared dreaming as home entertainment, you get to choose your category. Maybe it's not romance you're looking for tonight with that special person, but something more like an Indiana Jones movie, or the History Channel, or a sci-fi adventure with better special effects than even James Cameron has so far contrived. You can have that too, and the best thing is you don't have to remain a spectator: you and your friend get starring roles.

I have walked on the back of a golden cobra the size of a skyscraper with a special friend to gain access to a very special library dedicated to a goddess of ancient Egypt. I have shared excellent adventures in conscious shared dreaming with other friends and partners in which we crossed time to visit the Viscontis in Renaissance Italy, when they were using the earliest hand-painted Tarot cards to work magic; entered into a world of Forest People — animate, talking trees; and visited a possible future in which an order of priestess-scientists is seeking to repair our world.

Want to try this? Do you have a partner or friend who is willing to play? If that person lives with you or near you, you can make a date to start out next to each other, in the bed or, anyway, close by. If you are intimate partners, you may find that tender lovemaking gives you the juice for a shared journey to the moon and stars — if both of you can stay awake or at least remember what happens in your dreams if you fall asleep.

But shared dreaming doesn't require you to start out from the same place or even on the same continent. And unless it's part of your agenda, sex is not required.

EXERCISE FOR PARTNERS

Making a Dream Date

To keep this simple, let's assume you have a friend who is not physically present with whom you'd like to share a dream adventure. You can set up your date like this:

1. Make the Date.

You might simply agree to try to meet in your dreams on, say, Wednesday night. Or you might be more time-specific, saying to each other "midnight Pacific time" or "between one and five AM."

2. Agree on a Rendezvous.

If you're new to this kind of thing, it's probably best to start out with a place in the physical world that one or both of you know. That café in Soho, that beach on Kauai, that stand of poplars in the Smoky Mountains. When you've acquired some practice, you can set your sights on locations in this world that neither of you have visited and locations beyond this world.

3. Make Sure You Agree on a Juicy Intention.

The idea of simply hanging out with your partner in a delightful locale — and not having to pay for the plane ticket or the five-star hotel suite — may be juicy enough. But there may be something even more compelling the two of you would like to do, from figuring out how to get the house loan to swimming with mermaids or spending the night locked in a tantric embrace. Whatever your agenda, make sure it is exciting. The energy of a juicy intention will help you to get there.

4. Make Your Intention Firm.

This means that, before going to bed, you'll write down and mentally affirm your intention to keep your rendezvous and pursue any further agenda you have agreed on with your partner.

5. Record Your Experiences.

Write down whatever your remember from the night of your assignation, whether or not it seems remotely relevant to your intention.

6. Share.

Give your partner your raw report, unedited and uncensored.

When you share, be alert to the time-slip phenomenon. When we go dreaming, we step outside linear time — unless we are versed in the art of traveling close to "real time" in order to track physical situations very closely. We are capable of having shared experiences that are simultaneous in Dreamtime but are recollected at widely differing times (hours, days, or even weeks or more apart) in serial time. So if your reports from the night of your rendezvous do not match up as closely as you would like, be open to the possibility that one of you may have recalled your shared experience earlier or later than the other — perhaps even before the experiment was begun.

Shared dreaming is not only wonderful fun but can also help us on the roads of everyday life. It can save your job. Consider the following true-life narrative involving a couple I know well.

How Shared Dreaming Saved George's Job

George, a senior executive, dreamed he received an urgent summons from one of his bosses to meet that boss at his second home on the beach. George woke with the sinking feeling that he had just been canned.

When he shared this dream at one of my workshops, which he was attending with his wife, I suggested that, if it were my dream, I would want to go back inside it and get some more specific information via the dream reentry technique. I told George that he could ask another person in the workshop to go inside the dream with him and act as tracker — gathering information for him from an independent perspective — in an exercise in conscious shared dreaming in which we would use shamanic drumming to fuel and focus the journey.

George was excited by this plan. He invited his wife to be his partner and tracker. At the end of my drumming, they were eager to share their reports. They described the boss's beach home as if they had inspected it with a real estate agent. Being a guy, George had spent more time looking at the den and the deck than at the kitchen and the closets, but their accounts — of a place neither had ever seen outside their shared dreaming — were remarkably similar.

They returned with far more than the layout of the beach house. They now had information on a crisis brewing behind the scenes in George's organization that, he realized, could definitely cost him his job unless he made certain moves, fast. He acted on this data gleaned from shared dreaming. The upshot was that, when he was summoned to his boss's beach house for a crisis meeting six months later, he did not have to ask the way to the bathroom, since he had already been there in his conscious dream. And he was sitting on the right side of the table — with those who had kept their jobs and had to tell others about downsizing — because of the action he had taken with the information gained in his shared dreaming.

Here's the process George and his wife followed in order to enter his dreamspace together, share an adventure, and bring back the knowledge that saved his job.

EXERCISE FOR TWO OR MORE PARTNERS

Dream Reentry and Tracking

Phase 1. Tell the Dream.

The dreamer tells the dream as simply and clearly as possible.

Phase 2. Discuss.

The tracker may ask a few questions to get a clearer picture.

Before the journey, the tracker should ask the dreamer two key questions:

A.   What do you want to know?

B.   What do you intend to *do* inside the dream?

The dreamer then formulates the dual intention for the journey. For example: (1) I want to know why a bear is trying to get in my front door, and (2) I will face the bear and see if it has a message or gift for me.

Phase 3. Journey into the Dream.

The tracker asks permission to enter the dreamer's space to pursue the agreed-upon intention.

Partners may want to lie (or sit) so they are touching lightly during the journey.

Use a drumming CD for the journey.

Phase 4. Share Travel Reports.

Take a quiet moment to make notes from the journey.

The tracker speaks first. The correct form is to say, "In my dream of your dream…"

The dreamer gives his travel report.

Phase 5. Come Up with an Action Plan.

The tracker asks the dreamer, "How are you going to honor this experience?"

The exercise is not complete until the dreamer has decided on a definite action plan.

Adventures in Group Dreaming

To give you more of a feel for what is possible in conscious shared dreaming with one or more partners, I'll share some experiences from a single day at a workshop I led in Boulder, Colorado.

A Swiss woman in the group shared a dream in which she is on the deck of a cruise ship at night. The moon grows bigger and bigger until it fills half the sky, to the right of the boat. As she nears the moon, she is amazed and thrilled to see that it is covered with lush green vegetation that reminds her of scenes from her childhood in the French part of Switzerland. She is eager to reenter this dream, and so, of course, are we.

We set our intention to travel together and explore this moon of grass. People arrange themselves comfortably in the space, and I drum to fuel the journey. I find it unusually difficult to enter the dreamscape as it was described to us. I can get on the cruise ship easily enough and feel the rhythms of the waves. But however hard I try, I cannot visualize the moon on the *right* side of the boat; it continues to hang in the sky on the left. So I try a path I have used before, the path of moonlight on water. Now the moon of my vision is straight ahead, across the ocean, laying a path of light along which I travel into the realm of Luna. There is no sign of the lush green vegetation the dreamer described. Instead, I see locales familiar to me from previous journeys. Something inspires me to go *through* this lunar scenery. I travel rapidly through a series of doors and passages and come out in a lush green garden on the other side of the moon. The high grass and the flowering trees are full of eyes, the eyes of boys and girls who are living here. I understand that this is a place of lost children who came here when the world was too much (or too little). I think about how to bring them home to the grown-ups in the world who are missing their beautiful moon children. As I turn around, I see that the moon — the moon of grass — is now on my right.

The Swiss dreamer's report of her own journey was extraordinary. In the realm of the moon, she found a tool of vision: an abalone shell filled with water. As she looked in this mirror of water, she saw a second self looking in an abalone shell — at another, smaller self, looking at a yet smaller version…and so on, all the way down, maybe into infinity. Then she sensed a larger self, viewing her in a mirror of water…and so on, all the way up, perhaps into infinity. From this lovely and simple vision of nested realities, her consciousness expanded and she began to perceive the possible shape of the multiverse.

Later in the Boulder workshop, I was privileged to work with a Navajo elder named Abraham, who had driven up from Flagstaff because he had heard that I dream in the way of the ancestors and can teach others to do that. He wanted to reenter a dream from many years ago. He told the smaller group of dream trackers we formed for this exploration that, in 1984, he had dreamed he was riding a paint across the desert with his deceased grandfather and a family friend who had also passed on. They were riding hard toward a great rounded sandstone boulder rising above the dunes. He knew there were important teachings to be received at this place. But the dream had been interrupted, and he had been unable to get back to that place.

When I drummed for the journey, I enjoyed galloping across the desert on a cream horse with a white mane. Rattlesnakes sounded a warning as I neared the great sandstone boulder. I could see no obvious way either to enter the sandstone boulder — using it as a portal — or to move beyond it. I began to feel that perhaps this was sacred territory reserved for the Navajo, and that I was not welcome in it. Then I sensed something above me and looked up to find a giant eagle — an eagle as big as a mountain — hovering overhead. Its wings were striped in horizontal bands of bright rainbow colors. I looked down at the ground and saw the same rainbow eagle depicted in a sand painting at my feet. In that moment, I realized I had stepped through the sandstone portal and been received into a Navajo imaginal world. I walked by water and saw Abraham walking there, too, with an animal ally at his heel. I heard the long blessing-way chants of his grandfather and witnessed some indigenous ways of healing.

When we shared journey reports, the deep grooves on Abraham's face opened into a smile of delight as I described the rainbow eagle. He proceeded to tell us how he had found a place of sacred teaching and healing by water, inside the world of the sandstone boulder, and had been followed everywhere by a Gila monster — regarded by his people as a great diagnostician — that he would now work with, consciously, as an ally in healing work. He pronounced *Gila* the Spanish way, so it sounded like he was speaking of a "healer monster."

Later I was privileged to have Abraham as one of my trackers when I shared a dream about a Saturday night when, on my way to giving a lecture on Sir William Johnson and the Iroquois in a huge auditorium, I found myself on top of a soaring mountain, inside a security fence, and had to jump down in order to give my presentation. Abraham saw the mountain becoming an eagle, and the area at the crest within the security fence as the head of a bald eagle, and then saw the mountain-sized eagle wrapping itself around me to guide and protect me. Thea, another of my trackers, had a very down-to-earth vision of my dream. She advised me to remember "not to make mountains out of molehills" and to remember to "come down to earth" in order to reach all my audiences where they live. I loved both messages, which were nicely balanced and again demonstrated how we always benefit from multiple perspectives on our dream material.

The next example of shamanic group dreaming comes from a workshop I led on Cortes Island in British Columbia.

Rescuing the Lost Children from the Glass Bubble

I am out in the woods in the middle of the night. I notice other figures, animal and human and hybrid, moving among the trees, taking form then fading back into the shadows. I find three clear and reliable travel companions. Red-Tailed Hawk scouts ahead, Gray Wolf flanks me on the left, Bear advances on my right.

We come to the crest of a hill. Now the scene is open. There is a building in the distance, modern in style, with huge glass doors under sweeping arches. On the right side of the grassy hill is a huge glass dome. Inside, young children are playing, at least twenty of them, aged from perhaps two to eleven, both boys and girls. They seem unaware of the world outside their glass bubble. I wonder if the inside surface of the glass is treated so they can't see out — mirrored, or presenting the semblance of solid walls or a different landscape.

I have the clear sense that the kids in the bubble are the child selves of adults I'm working with. I'll need to discover how to get them out without scaring them by shattering the glass.

This was my record from a conscious dream. I had asked for a dream to guide the group I was leading in a depth adventure in Active Dreaming at beautiful Hollyhock, a retreat center on Cortes Island.

I shared the dream with my group after opening the workshop the following day. There was a stir of excitement when I proposed that we all enter the dreamscape, with the help of shamanic drumming, in a conscious group journey to investigate whether some of our lost boys and girls were inside the glass dome, and if so, how we could release them to reclaim their vital energy and imagination in our lives.

Before we embarked on the group expedition, I invited the twenty dreamers in our circle to recruit their own animal guardians to assist them on their missions, though Hawk and Wolf and Bear would be available to all. We spent a little time discussing the nature of soul loss — how we are liable to lose parts of our vital energy and identity in life through pain or shame or confinement or wrenching life choices — and how a form of negotiation is often required to reclaim a child self who has gone missing. The wounded child who may have "checked out" during an early passage in life because the world was too lonely or too cruel will need to be reassured that we are safe and also fun to be around.

A further agreed-upon intention for the group journey was to explore what was in the intriguing building beyond the glass dome.

The group expedition was wonderfully deep and vivid and healing for all. The preferred mode of access to the bubble was to tunnel underneath. My bear ally used his huge paws like earthmoving equipment, and then I found that the hard, flat bottom could be slid open as if the dome were a giant snow globe. Three younger versions of myself appeared as helpers. I don't think they were with the lost children in the bubble; I think they had companioned me unnoticed till it was time to assist the other children. I was moved to tears by the intrepid operations of these young Roberts, who found other kids and helped to persuade them that their adult selves were safe and could even be *fun.*

When I entered the building beyond the dome, I found its center was a magnificent room with a vaulted ceiling where a fountain spurted at least two stories into the air. The room filled with eager children who gathered around the figure of Old Grandfather Storyteller, who told the most wonderful tales, making it clear that keeping our inner children present will involve telling and living better stories — stories they want to hear and to which they can contribute. This was a beautiful and powerful shared adventure in Active Dreaming. The stories of the twenty dreamers who found younger selves in the giant snow globe all spoke of deep soul-recovery healing.

This is an example of shamanic lucid dreaming by a group of active dreamers. The success of our expedition was based on three simple things, already noted as the prerequisites for conscious dream travel. First, we had a portal, the gateway image of the glass dome containing the children. It helped that this was not part of a prefabricated script but a fresh image that had come to me on behalf of the group. Second, we developed a clear intention: to enter the dreamscape together and seek to rescue our lost boys and girls. Third, we had fuel for our group journey, not only the shamanic drumming but also the deep energy of the circle, which we had grown over the previous days of the workshop.

I must add that we had also made previous group journeys to connect or reconnect with animal guardians. As noted, the shamanic dreamer works with spiritual allies that often appear in the form of birds and animals. In part 2 of this book, you will find a simple and fun exercise that will put you in touch with your power animals as you construct a personal energy map.

PART 2

Active Dreaming for Conscious Living

If you haven't the strength to impose your own terms upon life, you must accept the terms it offers you.

— T. S. ELIOT

7

Rescuing Our Lost Children

Our most potent muse is our inner child.

— STEPHEN NACHMANOVITCH, *Free Play*

We are ready to learn how to approach waking life as a conscious dream, in the spirit of play. We will find, once again, that the master teacher is no stranger.

"The creative mind plays with the objects it loves," said Carl Jung.[10] An earnest man at one of my lectures once asked me to summarize what I consider essential practice. I said, "Remember to play." He carefully wrote down those three words as if he were marking a schedule. I don't think he quite got the message.

The child inside him — and in each of us — knows. Like puppies or lion cubs or dolphins spinning silver lariats of bubbles, children play for the joy of playing. Young children are masters of imagination, since they know the magic of making things up. Our first and best teacher of conscious living is our inner child.

But that inner child may have gone into hiding, under a glass dome or in a room in Grandma's house, because of shame or abuse, ridicule or loneliness, because the world wasn't safe or it wasn't fun. If we have lost our dreams, if our imagination is stuck in a groove, it's because we have lost our inner child. To live as active dreamers in everyday life, we have to bring that child home. This requires a quest, a negotiation, and fulfillment of a promise.

The quest will lead us down halls of memory to a place and time where our wonder child went missing. We can embark on the quest as a guided journey (via an exercise at the end of this chapter) to a real place in the imaginal realm.

The negotiation requires us to convince our child selves that we are safe and we are fun to be around. Fulfilling the promises we make will require us to remember to play without scheduling it.

Play first, work later, our child selves will insist. The cautious, dutiful adult self will protest. But if we are to keep our inner children at home in our bodies and our lives, we'll need to fulfill our promises to be fun as well as safe. If we play well enough, then before we quite know it, we'll fall in love with our work because it will be our play.

Of Floating and Childish Things

Whenever I go to Evanston, Illinois, I like to walk the path along Lake Michigan up to what I call the Northwestern Message Board. This is a grand jumble of cement slabs and boulders behind the Northwestern University campus that the kids have adorned with the colors of their imaginations. You feel young hearts beating and hopes running high. While some of the painted messages are out of the Hallmark greeting card aisle — "I will love you forever," "True love never dies" — some, whether borrowed or original, are infused with freshness and wonder.

It was raining hard as I followed the lakeshore path under the hood of a light windbreaker, but my heart still leaped when I saw the first signal from the message board: "COUNT ME IN," painted on a slab in big bold letters. Following the path up onto a headland, behind a young girl wobbling along on a creaky purple bike, I found a slab with this message: "The reluctance to put away childish things may be a requirement of genius." The quote is a neat backhand swipe at Paul's injunction (in Corinthians 11:13) about the need for a man to "put away childish things." It's borrowed material, from journalist and writer Rebecca Pepper Sinkler, but a grand message for that or any day.

C.S. Lewis played with Paul's famous Bible phrase in a slightly different way while conveying a similar message: "To be concerned about being grown up, to admire the grown up because it is grown up, to blush at the suspicion of being childish; these things are the marks of childhood and adolescence. And in childhood and adolescence they are, in moderation, healthy symptoms. Young things ought to want to grow. But to carry on into middle life or even into early manhood this concern about being adult is a mark of really arrested development. When I was ten, I read fairy tales in secret and would have been ashamed if I had been found doing so. Now that I am fifty I read them openly. When I became a man I put away childish things, including the fear of childishness and the desire to be very grown up."[11]

I wondered what a man I had encountered the day before on the plane en route to Chicago's O'Hare airport would have made of this. As he tried to push through a crowded aisle, he said loudly: "Life is never easy. And it's never pleasant." I couldn't let this go. I looked up at him from my seat and said, "I do hope life gives you cause to change that opinion. Otherwise you may find that opinion walking ahead of you, giving you more and more reasons to believe it."

I walked farther along the lakeshore path and found a message I'll bet wasn't borrowed: "Randy, you are more radiant than tungsten." I wonder where *that* led. What we encounter in life depends so much on what we can imagine. I am certain that, if I go with the idea that I am "more radiant than tungsten," I will encounter — and attract — things on my life roads that are very different from the ones I'll attract if I insist on the mantra "Life is never easy and never pleasant."

In my Evanston workshop that weekend, a psychotherapist shared a dream in which she met two small people who had a planet to themselves, out among the stars. We were reminded of Saint-Exupéry's Little Prince. "Grown-ups never understand anything for themselves, and it is tiresome for children to be always and forever explaining things to them," we are told in that luminous book. The therapist shivered at the suggestion that the two small people on their lonely planet among the stars might want to come home to live with their adult selves in our world.

Bringing Home the Child Who Sees Colors

Dorothea Hover-Kramer is a gifted and caring psychotherapist who was conceived in Germany at the time Hitler was invading Poland. She grew up seeing the colors of people's energy fields and was almost over-whelmed by all the darkness she saw — while aged three and four — as the Nazi dream progressed toward Hitler's suicide in the bunker.

She was in Berlin when the Allies moved in, and recalls that the most light she had ever seen around a person was in the energy fields of some of the black American soldiers, the first black people to enter her life.

Her mother died in the wreckage of Berlin when Dorothea was only five. Alone with her sister, Dorothea recruited a refugee to look after them and cook for them, based on the colors of the woman's aura.

Later, struggling to make her way, she ceased to be able to see people's colors. The gift of reading "biofields" (as she learned to call them) revived only thirty years later when, as a nurse, she learned about thera-peutic touch and helped to develop the now international healing touch program twenty years ago.

Her story brings to mind all the other people (often survivors of much less extreme situations) who have been led to suppress or part company with that magical child in each of us who sees the colors of people's feelings and is at home in the worlds of imagination.

I think of a woman I know who was punished by her art teacher in elementary school because she persisted in drawing colors around peo-ple because that was what she saw. "It's not real!" her teacher screamed at her. "People don't have colors around them!" So that little girl stopped drawing colors, and fairly soon she stopped seeing them.

I recall drawing motion lines around the figures of humans and animals when I was a very young boy, even when they were depicted as sitting or standing still, because I saw energy patterns around them. To-day, mainstream science is confirming the reality of the human biofield.

In her book *Second Chance at Your Dream*, Dorothea describes a new technology whose slightly unsettling acronym is SQUID (for Superconducting Quantum Interference Device); it seems this can track the parameters of the human energy bubble.[12]

We must learn to make room in our lives for the child within us who sees colors or energy patterns and knows the magic of making things up. In that cause, we don't want to miss any chance to play adult kindergarten.

The Child's Other World

In a room overlooking Spring Street in New York's colorful SoHo district, I am drumming to help twenty-four dreamers call up the right dream to play with — or play with them — on a wintry Saturday morning. Everyone has sketch paper and crayons, because the first thing we'll do is turn the dream that comes up into an instant drawing. Adult kindergarten is great. It brings out the child in each of us who is a natural creator.

At the end of the drumming, I rough out my own picture. It shows a figure whose head and upper body are those of a giant salmon, and whose lower body is that of a woman. She is the Salmon Speaker. She has stepped through a holo-screen to lecture a council of world leaders on their responsibilities to water and all that lives in water. She is a being from Dreamland, the future society of my deeper dreaming, in which dreamers speak for the planet.

Other pictures are bursting to life all around me. It's time for introductions. I ask people to briefly introduce themselves by stating their names, their intentions in coming to the workshop (Writing from Dreams) and the titles — just the titles — of their dream pictures. I spin the drumstick to show us where to begin, inviting the play of coincidence. When coincidence is in play, a woman in the circle said to me earlier, "you feel the fingers of the universe are on you."

Some of the dream titles are so juicy and inviting that I pause the introductions more than once to have people meditate on a phrase or simply write a few lines from it, jotting down the first things that it releases in their minds. One of those irresistible titles is "The Child's Other World." The phrase transports all of us into places of memory and imagination, into an enchanted apple orchard or through a green door no one else can see.

In her child's other world, wrote Margaret, one of the participants, there is "the joy of touching, smelling, feeling, playing with, hiding in the sun-hot dark dirt between the strawberry plants of our big backyard, alone and breathing in the tangy grass."

In that other world, Yuliya found herself "floating on the clouds, very light, dissolving, feeling lifted into the sky." Miki found herself stepping through a dream door, "exiting a spaceship onto a planet where it is night, there are trees and hills on the horizon, but in front of me only a cleared space. To my left I can turn to a swing set, as yet motionless, and to my right is a stationary park bench. Everything is blue, including the light."

In the child's other world, Lori played "imaginary chess in the park." Lauraine found that the other world of children "is seen through the kaleidoscope of their eyes. The patterns and colors transfix them with the magical possibilities of the coming day. Flights of fancy, rainbows, and dreamscapes interweave seamlessly into the sidewalks, trees, and buildings around them."

For me, the Child's Other World is a world within this one. Its cloudy skies are the sheets I have pulled over my head as I lie in bed, aged nine or so. Grown-ups can't understand that the world inside the sheets is bigger than the one outside.

The Bazaar of Lost and Found Souls

Sometimes our inner child won't come home until we go in search of him or her. I've led many groups on quests that begin at a real location in the imaginal realm that I call the Magic Market. Its full name is the Bazaar of Lost and Found Souls. I invite you to travel this road if you are interested in bringing more of the joy and the creative play of your child self into your present life.

The Magic Market and the House of Gifts

You are approaching an outdoor market. You can picture this as a market you know. I often think of the famous Santa Fe Flea Market. The market is rich in scents and colors. There is fresh produce, spices, teas and soaps, beads and jewelry, crafts and clothing. You wander with delight among the stalls. Maybe you are drawn to the alley of the antiquarian book dealers, or a display of tribal masks, or the heirloom silver, or the bird sellers' corner.

Eventually you find yourself at a stall that is unlike the others. The items on display are oddly familiar to you. As you inspect them more closely, you realize these are all objects from your childhood. A doll or a game, a mirror or a toy soldier, a plastic submarine, a periscope, a teddy bear, or a piggy bank.

Each of these items holds memories and magic for you from your early childhood. You select just one of these objects. You pick it up and turn it around in your hands, inspecting it closely. You find that it is a key. Though it may look nothing like a key, this magic item from childhood has the power to open a door in a wall you didn't notice until now.

There, on the far side of the market, you now see a high wooden wall. From behind it emerges the sound of snorting and stamping, as of horses.

A door is opening in the wall, and a horse comes cantering out. This is your spirit horse, your ride for the journey that will now deepen. However you may feel about horses under other circumstances, you are completely at home with this horse. You spring effortlessly onto its back. Soon you are speeding — now flying — over a larger landscape.

In the distance, you see a huge tent arranged for some festivity, perhaps a wedding or a family reunion. This is your House of Gifts.

When your horse gets you there, you will find yourself entering a space in which you will recognize multiple aspects of yourself and your gifts. There may be a baby version of you, and a small child, and a teenager, and perhaps an adult version of you that went away when you made a life-wrenching choice that a part of you resisted.

Now is your opportunity to meet and negotiate with aspects of your energy and identity that may have gone missing from you as a result of life's bruises and disappointments. First and last, this is your chance to reclaim your inner child, the greatest of your muses. To do that, you'll have to promise to be safe and to be fun, and then you'll be required to deliver on that promise. You can start immediately by giving yourself a treat that five-year-old or nine-year-old you would enjoy, anything from blowing soap bubbles to a smoothie or running wild in the woods.

8

Reclaiming the Power of Naming

Everyone has their own sky
Everyone has their own trail.

— DAUR MONGOL SAYING

W hen I meet someone new, I like to ask him if he knows what his
name means. This is a way of registering the new person's name
in my mind so it doesn't slip. It's also a great conversation starter.

I find it interesting that lots of people, even at the midpoint of life
or beyond it, seem never to have paused to ask what their name means.
One of my workshops was hosted by a thoughtful couple in Maryland. I
put my question to them. The wife — Deborah — knew that her name
means "honeybee" in Hebrew. She did not know that it is also the name
of the priestess of the Great Goddess in very early times; *Deborah* has the
same double meaning ("honeybee" and "priestess") as *Melissa* in Greek.

The husband was another Robert. He didn't know what the name
means. It wasn't hard for me to help him out, since I've often had occasion to reflect on what my name means. It's of Scandinavian origin,
though it came down to me through my father's Scottish line (those Vi-
kings got around). The original meaning of *Robert* is "bright in fame."
There's a double edge for me in that. My name says to me: "Be ready for

the spotlight, and try to stay bright (in all senses) when it's on you." I've gone through such radical changes in my life that I might have thought of changing my name several times over to reflect the changes in me and my sense of what matters. But through all my life passages, *Robert* has felt like the right name for me. However, I won't tolerate any messing around with it. Call me Bob, and I become dangerous.

On the other hand, I know plenty of Bobs who aren't Roberts. It's interesting to notice what's being reflected or invoked energetically if we switch from the formal version of a name to a colloquial or abbreviated one or do the reverse. A Bob is not a Robert. A Betsy is not an Elizabeth. Betsy might be the fun and friendly lady next door, the perfect soccer mom, and short-order cook for the neighborhood kids. Elizabeth travels with a name that evokes royalty and sacred intent; her name literally means "the house of God."

The Egyptians regarded the name (*ren*) as an aspect of soul and believed that any assault on a person's name — for example, the defacement of an inscription — was an act of soul mutilation, even soul murder. At the start of my workshops, I ask everyone in the circle to begin by claiming his or her name and announcing it to the circle in a clear, ringing voice. "If you don't like the name you've been given or are called by others, change it now and we'll say it back to you."

What's in a Name Is You

What's in a name, first and last, is you. You want to know what your name means, and what gift or challenge is in that meaning. You want to be sure the name you are using suits your natural energy and is not like a suit two sizes too small and buttoned up tight, or a pair of shoes that are just too big for you.

The penalty for letting other people take your name and tell you who you are can be immense. Take the case of Charles, who was compelled to become Chuck.

Getting Chucked

"You can call me Charles for now," he told me. "But they're going to turn me into a Chuck."

Charles was a Southern gentleman working in one of the dark towers of Manhattan publishing. His courtly manners and mild accent, curling gently like tobacco leaf in the sun, belonged in a family firm or one of the smaller independent houses. But he was making *lots* of money at his giant company, turning the first drafts of certain brand-name commercial fiction into books that would make the authors appear better than dyslexic without overestimating the attention span of their readers. He reached to the side of his desk to show me a specimen, a typescript that had recently been delivered in a Rodeo Drive shopping bag. There were gaps on some pages where the author had run out of ideas. She had scribbled a note to her editors, signed with a lipstick kiss: "I trust you to fill me in."

I studied the editor, immaculate even in shirtsleeves, with his suspenders and discreet monogram stitched on his breast pocket. "You don't look like a Chuck," I said.

"I was never once called that. When I was a kid, some of my buddies called me Charlie, but never Chuck. But there's a Charles and a Charlie in the office, so they said I'll have to be Chuck."

"You can't let them take your name away," I protested. "That's identity theft. Once they've stolen your name, who knows what else they'll take?" I didn't know Charles very well, but I was going to say my piece. "The Egyptians said that the name is a part of the soul. If you deface someone's name, you murder something in his soul."

"The Egyptians, huh?"

"Listen, I'm going to be with you all the way on this. I'll insist on calling you Charles under all circumstances. You need to put up a fight."

"Well, I can try." He leaned back in the mock-leather executive swivel seat. Not yet a corner office, but the window behind him gave a clear view of the avenue and the giant upended ice cube tray on the other side. "But I don't think they'll let me get away with it."

I next called on Charles about three weeks later. When I gave his name to the blue uniform at the reception desk, the guard took his time studying a list before he declared, "There is no one by that name in this company."

"That's impossible. We have an appointment. I spoke to him on the phone yesterday. Why don't you call upstairs?"

He spoke to someone on the house phone, and then gave me the same answer. Nobody called Charles _____ worked at that publishing company.

An awful suspicion grew in me. I voiced it with great reluctance. "Will you see if there's a Mr. Chuck _____ ?"

The guard found Chuck on his list right away, gave me my visitor's badge, and sent me off to the elevator.

"I told you they wouldn't let me get away with it," Chuck told me when the door was closed.

I was curious to see what would happen next. Charles had scheduled two weeks of vacation time to work on a book of his own, which he modestly called "a little thing," reflections on a favorite pastime, like fly-fishing. His boss kept postponing his vacation. He spent that whole summer working in the city, and by the time the holidays came around he was too burned-out to work on his book.

He lasted much longer than might have been expected at a company whose employment pattern was described by junior staffers as "a revolving door." It was years before Charles, now Chuck, got chucked — laid off with a few weeks' notice. I heard he later found a job at a smaller company south of New York. I hope he got his name back, and I'd like to read his book some day.

Naming Your Demons

Every child remembers the story of Rumpelstiltskin, the strange little man in the Grimm's fairy tale who has power over the miller's daughter until she discovers his name. Just as we want to claim the power of naming ourselves, we need to find out the name of the Rumpelstiltskins in our lives: the personal demons who oppress us and bring us down.

Sometimes they show up like unwanted guests at the door to sap our confidence and suck the joy out of a day. I've invented a game that will enable you to name the unwelcome caller that steals your resolve and throws you off course. His name may be fear or rage or guilt. But it can also be a softer name with a better reputation, such as empathy

don't take time to be with her. I don't listen to her, and I don't allow her a larger space to create in.

I asked her if what I was working on pleased her. She said yes, but that she wanted this project to go in another direction, and I wasn't allowing her the time and space to do it.

I took her into a large room and we sat down. I took her hands in mine and blessed her hands, and my hands became hers.

So, she's back again. She went away angry out of neglect. I'm very sorry she left, but am glad she's back. My practice now is to look at her hands — my hands — before I start my creative work and ask her what she wants to do today. I don't want to lose her again.

Jennifer: Feeding Sadness Popcorn and Swedish Fish

Sadness greeted me. She looked like a washed-out version of myself. I invited her in and hugged her for a long time, giving her the energy of joy. Then we went over to the couch and popped in a funny movie to watch while nibbling on popcorn and Swedish Fish wine gum candies. We laughed out loud and sat close together.

My practice will be to snack on these things whenever I feel Sadness coming around again.

Carol: Grief Is a Stray Kitten I Don't Want to Leave

A small gray kitten is meowing at my door. "I am a slight grief," she says. "Let me in for a bit. I am a stray, and I don't play well with others." "Of course," I say, "come in and stay for what you need. I welcome companionship and you are quite sweet."

Grief is a complicated companion with many stories of hello and good-bye, and I suspect she is bigger than she looks. As we sit and sip cream, I realize how cozy it is to be with her, gently grieving what we have lost. When she gets up to leave, swishing her fluffy gray tail, I try to stop her. "Please don't go. Don't leave me alone."

"That's the point," says Grief. "I must leave so that you will *not* be alone."

Grief leaves on silent feet. I'm shocked at how I spoke to her. I'm left with a Zen riddle. Am I alone now, or not alone?

Michele: Anger Comes Dressed in Red

Anger shows up as a short stocky guy with ruddy skin, a red T-shirt, and long jean shorts. When I let him in (after he incessantly leans on the buzzer downstairs), he pounds up the stairs to my apartment. Puffed out, pissed off, he finds something wrong with everything I offer, and everyone in the world is annoying him.

I grab some paper and crayons and place them in front of him. Jabbing angrily at the paper at first, he eventually calms down. He leaves shortly after he arrives. But then, Anger never stays long.

He's such a humorous caricature for me that, hopefully, the next time I get mad I'll just laugh! Or maybe he'll leave even sooner. I love this game!

Janet: Inadequacy Can't Measure Up to Joy

Inadequacy shows up on my doorstep with my mother's face. I don't know how to help her, because she can't even decide if she wants a cup of coffee or not. I try to write my way through this, but my computer crashes — twice. Seems like I'm too inadequate even to write about Inadequacy.

I'm so frustrated I can't think of anything to do with her, until I notice a laughing young woman sitting on my desk next to the computer, winking at me. She looks like a younger version of me, with the body of a dancer. Her eyes sparkle with mischief.

"How long have *you* been here?"

"Long enough," she laughs, twirling around the room.

"Are you the one who stopped me from writing about Inadequacy?"

She nods and yells, "Screw Inadequacy! This is your year for Joy, and I am Joy in the bod, baby! It's time to embrace me. Oooh, remember *this*?"

I see two hummingbirds appear. She stands still, her face lifted toward the sun, rapturous, while the hummingbirds hover in the air over her shoulders. The wind from their wings blows back her hair.

I know this. It's from an old dream in which hummingbirds flew into a room and *chose* me and I felt blessed. But then I shooed them away because people were watching and I got embarrassed.

"You were chosen," says Joy. "You *are* chosen. Get up every day and look in the mirror and say, 'I have been chosen,' and believe it and revel in it. You've had a lot of years of entertaining Inadequacy. This is your time for Joy."

I get up and dance around the room with Joy and feel the wind of hummingbird wings. I choose Joy.

Robin: Resentment Putty

I turn into the drive, and there she is, oozing all over my front porch, like so much goopy slime. There's no mistaking her stench and that way she has of attaching herself to all the nooks and crannies — Resentment is here all right, and she didn't wait for me to meet her at the door.

I could just go in through the garage and avoid her altogether. Yes, this seems wise — goodness knows, she's not going anywhere. She can wait while I transition from being out and about to settling in at home.

I hang my keys, pet the puppy, take a quick look at the pile of dishes and crummy countertop no one else has bothered to clean up. I pick up a cereal box and milk carton. Harumph, they're both empty — of course, no one could just throw them away. And look, the friggin' garbage can is overflowing — can *no one* take it out? This is not rocket science — full can needs to go O-U-T.

Well, apparently Resentment isn't waiting for me to open the door and invite her in — she's found her way into my kitchen just fine. I see her scuzzy film coating the floor, her stinky essence permeating the air — she's in all the toilet bowls, laundry hampers, piles of bills, wilting flowers, and missing socks, keys, and power cords. Her presence intensifies in every unsaid accusation, unfinished conversation, unread book, unwritten story. She even thinks she can hide in piles underneath everyone's unmade beds. Guess that's what I get for avoiding her and putting her on hold — she just slathers her nasty ick that much thicker and deeper, until it's up to my chin.

She pummels my head as I stride purposefully up the stairs on a mission, only to realize once I get there that I've completely forgotten why I've come. Her cackling voice sneers and taunts me: "I'm he-e-e-e-ere, dearie. There's always room for me." Suddenly my beautiful sanctuary home feels like Gollum's dark, dank cave.

Ah, now I remember why I came up here! My laughter CD — the goofy fourteen-minute-long giggle cycle that comes on when I hit Play. I hit the button and — *Bahaha* — the laughs begin.

Laughter is to Resentment as water is to the Wicked Witch of the West. Resentment begins melting in mirth and goofy, giddy glee. The ooze of Resentment recedes into one small, confined blob — a blob I can hold in my hand, molding, stretching and poking, working it like a stress ball until I can walk past the messes and stains and search with a clear mind for the little plastic egg-shaped container that used to be in the toy box but has managed to find its way to the laundry room, along with last Sunday's newspaper. I take the sticky blob, press it hard against the funny papers, then stuff what is now Silly Putty into the egg-trap, toss it back into the toy box, and smile.

I have not yet heard anyone name one of the trickiest demons, the one that the desert fathers called Acedia (ah-SEE-dee-yah). This is the most deadly of the tribe of noonday demons, a dry dementor that sucks the juice and joy out of everything. He is so tricky that at one point he succeeded in getting the learned editors of the *Oxford English Dictionary* to declare him "obsolete," as he sniggered behind his cupped hand: "I'll be baaaack." Acedia's name is being heard again, thanks in part to a luminous memoir-cum-meditation by Kathleen Norris titled *Acedia & Me.*

Acedia literally means "not-caring." Let's note that our word *care* derives from an Indo-European root meaning "to cry out." Not to care is not to cry out in the midst of life and death, to be perennially numb. Acedia produces a state of torpor and disaffection more serious than depression. Norris contends that, while depression is an illness that can be treated, acedia is a "vice" that can only be contained by spiritual practice and prayer.[14]

The next time he shows up at my door, I'll see how he needs to be handled and will report back — assuming I succeed and therefore still care.

Overcoming the Fifth Fear

I used to find it curious that the Buddhists define speaking in public as one of the five fears that constrain humans and stand between us and our freedom. "Fear of speaking before an assembly" is right up there with fear of death, fear of loss of livelihood, fear of loss of reputation, and fear of unusual states of mind.[15] Having worked with thousands of people in seminars and playshops where they are required to say their piece in front of others, I see that this fear is widespread and goes deep. It is often rooted in a family tradition of not speaking up, and in ancestral memories of times when it wasn't safe to speak truth before power.

To overcome the fifth fear, we must learn to define and explain ourselves before others. This is essential, because the human being is an animal that must define itself or be defined by others.

"Man is the most fortunate of all creatures," declared Giovanni Pico della Mirandola, the great Renaissance humanist, because God made him "a creature of indeterminate and indifferent nature" and said to him:

> Adam, we give you no fixed place to live, no form that is peculiar to you, nor any function that is yours alone. According to your desires and judgment, you will have and possess whatever place to live, whatever form, and whatever functions you yourself choose. All other things have a limited and fixed nature prescribed and bounded by our laws. You, with no limit or no bound, may choose for yourself the limits and bounds of your nature.
>
> We have placed you at the world's center so that you may survey everything else in the world. We have made you neither of heavenly nor of earthly stuff, neither mortal nor immortal, so that with free choice and dignity, you may fashion yourself into whatever form you choose. To you is granted the power of degrading yourself into the lower forms of life, the beasts, and to you is granted the power, contained in your intellect and judgment, to be reborn into the higher forms, the divine.[16]

This magnificent challenge echoes down the centuries. Active dreamers rise to meet it every day. We learn to name and define ourselves and our life projects, and to make ourselves heard and received by others and the listening universe. This requires us to overcome the fifth fear. Here are three practices that help.

PRACTICE 1

Define Your Personal Truth

Give yourself enough private time and space to respond to the following questions from deep inside, from your heart and your gut, not merely your head. Say them aloud in your own voice, then repeat them silently until the response wells up from within you:

- What do I love?
- What makes me happy?
- What does my heart long for?
- What would I risk everything to defend?
- If my life ended today, what would I most regret not having done?

Write down your responses. If you find you can't answer one of the questions, jot that one down, leaving it as a space in your mind and your life that will be filled when you have learned and grown more.

PRACTICE 2

Name Your Life Intention

When you have answered the questions in the previous exercise, you are ready to respond to the question that the American poet Mary Oliver expressed in "The Summer Day": "Tell me, what is it you plan to do with your one wild and precious life?"

So much in life depends on intention. It's time to come up with a big one.

Quick — what is your life intention?

I heard these responses at one of my workshops:

- I want to live every day as an adventure.
- I want to love and be loved.
- I want to be a healer.
- I want to bring something new into the world.
- I want to fulfill my sacred contract.
- I want to find my soul mate.
- I want to write children's books.
- I want to live my bigger story.

Whatever words you choose, they should pass the tingle test: they should give you goose bumps. However you state your life intention, the universe won't believe you until you come up with an action plan that supports it, starting with one simple physical action you can take right away. Personal truth is what we remember and act upon.

PRACTICE 3

Recruit Creative Friends

When you have defined your life purpose and have an action plan that serves it, you have a story that can travel. You're ready to start recruiting creative friends. A creative friend is someone who recognizes your need to live your bigger story and is willing to support you as you change and grow. Sometimes those who are closest to us have a really hard time with this, because they want us to stay the same, like the "picture in a frame" of a maudlin old love song.

We may need patience and cunning to bring along some old friends and loved ones who are scared of change. We may also want to recruit some new creative allies. In that cause, we need to be able to explain ourselves.

Practice coming up with two simple statements that you can use to introduce yourself.

In the first statement, you'll say something about your regular life. For example: "I'm Jill. I'm a software designer. I live in Evanston. I'm a single mother, and I love to go dancing."

Second, make a statement that reflects your life intention and/or the action plan that flows from it. Make this statement in the present tense and let it be wholly affirmative. Say it so anyone hearing you might be inspired to help. "I'm writing children's stories, and I'm always looking for new ideas." Or "I'm redecorating a barn where I'm going to paint." Or "I'm trying to live my bigger story."

When you have your statements clear and crisp, try both of them out on new acquaintances. Try the second one out on friends who may not have caught up with you, who may not recognize your intentions and where you have traveled in your life. You may be pleasantly surprised by how much helpful support you'll enlist when you present yourself and your life project this way. If your heart is in your words, the impact can be viral.

9

MAPPING THE NATURAL PATH
OF YOUR ENERGY

Energy is an eternal delight, and he who desires,
but acts not, breeds pestilence.

—— WILLIAM BLAKE

We must follow the natural path of our energy. Our bodies will show us, if we are sufficiently in touch with them. When we are at odds with our bodies, our dreams may supply the necessary course correction, if we are listening. Then there are ways to "MapQuest" our natural energy paths via active imagination.

One of my favorites is the conscious journey through the energy centers, as explained in this chapter. Yoga and Eastern medicine have worked for millennia with energy centers that are believed to pattern movements of the life force between the subtle body and the physical body. They are called chakras, or "wheels of light," in India because, in clairvoyant sight, the energy centers are often seen as revolving and vibrating. The movement of these centers is said to weave the fabric of the energy body, which surrounds the physical body and provides the template for symptoms and conditions registered on physical levels. There is some iconographic evidence that the Egyptians recognized similar energy centers. A simple approach to the chakras, focused on seven principal energy centers, has become increasingly popular in the West through the work of medical intuitives such as Carolyn Myss.

A self-scan of the energy centers is a wonderful tool for self-diagnosis, if we can find the way to perform the scan with sufficient detachment, which is a difficult thing for most of us to accomplish without a deep shift in consciousness. If we *can* manage that shift, we can open a path to self-healing. As Carolyn Myss advises, working with the subtle body through the energy centers is a noninvasive form of healing with tremendous potential to bring greater balance and reprogram the physical body so it rejects negative symptoms and intrusions.[17]

The journey through the energy centers, as explained here, facilitates the deep shift in consciousness that is required for accurate self-diagnosis and takes us far beyond diagnosis into realms of healing and empowerment. The journey opens gateways for soul recovery and the release of life blockages. It introduces and strengthens connections with the animal guardians and brings their vitality, tracking skills, and healing energies richly alive in the body. It encourages spontaneous art and creativity and offers rich personal mythology, which is healing in itself. Properly conducted, the journey raises a tremendous amount of life force and channels the movement of that energy into harmonious, unrestricted flow.

I make the journey through the energy centers myself at least every couple of weeks, and I never fail to be juiced by it and to learn new and important things from which I draw healing and guidance for myself and others. The living symbols and animal guardians I have come to know well are never still; they are constantly interacting, moving, and transforming, offering surprises and fresh gifts, and helping me to address new challenges.

The Active Dreaming approach to chakra work is different from yoga. You will be helped to enter, in a state of conscious dreaming, seven distinct spaces associated with the seven major chakras that are commonly recognized. In each of these spaces, you'll encounter gifts and challenges. In the course of the journey, you'll gather the symbols and images to produce a personal energy chart that looks like a totem pole of the Pacific Northwest, a *living* totem pole.

You will also learn how to make a second journey for self-healing, and how to make this journey with a partner as a shared experience of conscious dreaming for mutual healing.

Diagnostic Journey through the Energy Centers

We are about to embark on a gentle but profound journey through the energy centers. In the course of the journey, we will open emotional and spiritual landscapes that we can explore for self-understanding and self-healing. Where we find challenge or blockage, we can learn to operate within these spiritual landscapes to restore balance and natural flow. As we operate with intention within the landscapes of the energy centers, we can help to guide our bodies in the direction of wellness.

As we travel through the energy centers, we will encounter animal guardians and other life-forms associated with each of the centers. We will discover living symbols and spiritual helpers who can assist us in self-healing and who may help us to extend gifts of healing to others. Sometimes the animal forms and symbols we encounter will correspond to traditional visions of the colors and patterns of the chakras; often what we perceive will be fresh and new, with the individuality and power of a *big* dream coming to us from a place deeper than the controlling everyday mind. These fresh, spontaneous images often contain the deepest potential for healing, since they are intimately related to our life stories as they are recorded in our energy fields and enacted in our physical bodies. By working with these personal, unedited images, we can move through the mind-body connection to help the body shrug off unwanted symptoms and begin to become healthy.

Chances are, as you make this journey you will come to points of blockage or fear or confusion. Maybe you'll move to a particular energy center and find that there is nothing there, or everything is in darkness, or the passage is blocked. Locating these areas of blockage or challenge can be a profound gift. By identifying the problem areas and moving to release the blockage or resolve the challenge by using the techniques I will introduce later, you can move decisively toward healing. The moment of recognition is a point of power. If you can see what is blocking you — and where in your energy system that block is, and what part of your life story has produced it — you are more than halfway to releasing that block.

In the same way, if you find a gaping void in one of your energy centers, or find that the space there is cramped, or that the life-forms are sickly or undeveloped, this vision may also be a tremendous gift. One of the things often revealed in a deep journey through the energy centers is the reality and consequences of soul loss. If you find a void in your heart, you may be awakening to the fact that you lost a vital part of your energy — and with it your ability to experience and share love and trust — through heartbreak, grief, or trauma. The hole in your heart is probably begging to be filled. Your vision of that space at your heart may be an invitation to call back lost soul energy — perhaps a vital piece of you that went missing at an earlier time in your life — and let it live where it belongs, in your heart and your life.

If you find a hole in your solar plexus — perhaps a landscape devoid of life, or sunk in darkness, or consumed by a raging fire — this may be an invitation to reclaim your animal spirits and to harness the primal power of your passions, the fire that belongs in your belly. For shamans, the solar plexus, more than any other energy center, is the home of the animal guardians. If you do not find a strong animal form in your solar plexus, you need one. If you find emptiness or weakness here, you are being invited to claim an energy connection that will take you into the realm of the animal helpers.

You will be journeying through your own energy system, but no man is an island, and our energy fields intersect and overlap with those of other beings, human and nonhuman.

So your journey will prove to be both intensely personal and transpersonal. This will be clear to you as soon as you go deep into the realm of the animal powers, as you are bound to do when the landscapes of your energy centers open to you fully. The animals you find in your energy centers may have rich symbolic significance. The snake may represent your power of regeneration, your ability to shed the skin of your past life and raise the deep force of kundalini in your body and your awareness. The hummingbird may evoke your ability to heal the heart or find balance and stillness in the midst of perpetual motion. At the same time, the animal powers you find in your energy system may be living energy forms that can operate both within and outside your own body and are related to the life force of other species, your counterparts, or helpers in nature.

As you travel the energy centers, you will also encounter scenes and presences that reflect your connections with other humans, living and departed. You may detect energy "cords," or attachments, that link you to other people, and you will need to determine whether these attachments are healthy or otherwise — and if they are unhealthy, how to cut them.

As you rise through the higher energy centers, you will probably perceive symbols and presences that represent your connection with higher spiritual guidance and past-life experiences. At the crown center, which is the portal to transcendent experience of the spiritual realms, you may find yourself in contact with sacred beings — gods and goddesses, angels, and spiritual teachers — who support you on your life path. By opening to them more fully — always with discernment and discrimination — you may bring through immense light, clarity, and energy for your soul's journey in this life experience.

In the *goaded* meditation that follows, I give only a brief description of each of the energy centers and avoid describing colors or symbols traditionally associated with the chakras in ancient systems. The aim is to release you to use your own power of visioning to see things in fresh and personal ways, instead of having you constantly be told by the tour guide where to look and how to see things.

From this journey, you can construct your personal totem pole, a set of living images that can help you draw on sources of power and healing and awaken you to your larger identity and the deeper story of your life.

EXERCISE

Exploring Your Energy Body

Have drawing paper and crayons or markers ready to draw the images that come to you. On your seven-stage journey, you will pause after visiting each of the energy centers to draw a living symbol — perhaps an animal guardian — that appeared to you in that space. Start at the *bottom* of your paper, with an image from the root center. Add successive images one above the other until your "Living Totem Pole" is complete, with seven symbols.

For this journey, it is best to sit in a relaxed position with your spine fairly straight.

Take a few deep breaths and focus on relaxing into the flow of your breathing. If you are holding tension in any part of your body, tense and release the muscle groups associated with that part of the body and see if you can let the tension flow away.

Now focus on your intention. Your intention is to make a healing journey to the energy centers of your body. At each center, you will allow a scene to open, in which you will find an animal guardian or living symbol that will offer you guidance and power.

First Chakra: The Root Center

We are ready to embark on the journey. You are going deep, deep down, into the depths of your body and energy system. You are going down to your root center, at the base of your spine. In relation to your physical body, your root center is located at the perineum, between the sex organs and the anus. But you may find that your root center extends all the way down to the soles of your feet, and even down into the earth itself.

Your awareness is moving into your root center.

You may have an impression of color. What color is coming through?

You have an impression of an emerging shape or landscape. It may seem dark or blurry at first, but as you let yourself go deeper you find this space at the root center is opening out into a scene.

What is the landscape you find at your root center? Go into it. It may be opening before you like a cavern.

There is a life-form in this space. You can feel it stirring. Now you are beginning to perceive it more clearly. What is the animal or life-form you find in the space of your root center? Observe its behavior and condition. Is it strong? Is it healthy? Does it have the room it needs? Is there something missing or lacking here, something that isn't right?

Feel yourself going even deeper, all the way down into the earth. Is your connection to the earth open and strong? What is growing here, or failing to thrive?

You may pause at this point to draw the image of the animal or life-form you found at the root center. Draw this at the bottom of a piece of paper. This is the first image on your Living Totem Pole.

Second Chakra: Sex-Creative Center, Place of Birthing

Now you are ready to move from the root center up to your second chakra. This corresponds to your lower abdomen, between your sex organs and your belly. This is the center of active sexuality, birthing, and creativity.

As you approach this center, you may have a sense of color. The color may change as the center opens into a landscape or seascape.

You are entering the scene that is unfolding at your second energy center. Let it deepen. Explore it with all of your inner senses. What do you find? What lives here?

Is there an animal in the space of your sex center, your place of birthing? What animal is it? Observe its condition and its movements. Is it happy and strong, or does it need tending and nourishing?

Draw the image of the animal or life-form you encountered at your second chakra above the figure from your root center. This is the second image on your Living Totem Pole.

Third Chakra: Powerhouse

You are ready to go up to your solar plexus. This powerful energy center corresponds to the area between your navel and the base of your rib cage.

As you approach the solar plexus, you may have a sense of color. You may also have an impression of warmth or heat.

As you enter this power center, the space opens out and you find yourself moving into a landscape. The scene before you may be vast. Go deeper into it, look around in all directions, explore with all your inner senses.

There are life-forms — perhaps *many* life-forms — living and moving in the landscape that is unfolding around you. What animal or animals do you see? Observe their condition and behavior.

If you do *not* find an animal in the space of the solar plexus, or if the animal you find seems weak or sickly, pay special attention. The absence of strong animal energy at the solar plexus usually denotes major energy loss and is an invitation to reclaim your power.

Draw the third image on your Living Totem Pole, above the first two.

Fourth Chakra: Heart Center

You are ready for a *big* ascent, from the lower energy centers up to the heart center. Start by placing a hand over your physical heart. Give thanks to your heart for sustaining your life, for surviving all the burdens and trials that it has endured. Now move your hand a little to the right. You are getting in touch with your heart center. This is the center of love, of joy and sorrow, of courage, and of the thinking of the heart, which is wiser than the thinking of the head.

You have an impression of color, or colors, and perhaps a sense of warmth.

If you feel there are things blocking or covering your heart, let those blocks or coverings fall away. You are opening your heart.

Let yourself flow gently into the space of your heart center. Is it light or dark? Is it roomy or cramped?

Move deeper in. Let the space open out. You are expanding your awareness to encompass the whole space corresponding to your heart and lungs.

Breathe deeply as you continue to explore.

What life-forms or living symbols do you find in your heart center? Are there birds or animals? Do you find the faces of loved ones or sacred teachers? Do you find plants or flowers growing in the space of your heart?

If you find emptiness at your heart center, a void or something like an empty room, you are receiving an invitation to healing by means of soul recovery. A vacancy at the heart may suggest major soul loss via heartbreak, grief, or trauma. It also suggests a space that is ready to be filled with bright energy — the energy of returning younger selves and the radiant energy of the Higher Self.

Draw the symbol of your heart center on your Living Totem Pole, at the center of the page.

Fifth Chakra: Throat Center, Voice Box

Now you are ready to go up to the throat center. You may want to press your fingers gently against the base of your neck. As you do so, you approach your voice center, the center of communication and self-expression. You may want to hum or tone lightly as you approach this center, and let the resonance carry you deeper. This is a place of *sound* and vibration. Experiment until you find yourself making the right sound.

As you focus on your throat center, do you have a sense of color?

Let the space begin to open out. Maybe you have an impression of a passage or doorway. Let yourself move through it into a deeper space. What kind of scenery is emerging? Is there a life-form — bird or animal or something else — that appears to you in this space?

If you find yourself blocked or constricted, study the nature of the blockage or constriction. See if you can pull up a clear picture of the block. If that isn't possible, consider how the blockage or constriction *feels.* For example, does it feel like something is choking you or pressing into your neck?

Gather up your impressions.

Draw the image you found at your throat center on your Living Totem Pole, above the heart symbol. If you were blocked, draw an image of the block on the left side of your piece of paper. You'll come back and work on clearing this later.

Sixth Chakra: Third Eye, Vision Center

You are ready to go up to the third eye area, between and above your physical eyes, where Hindus place a dot. You may want to feel for this

place on your forehead with your fingertip. This is the center or vision
— of intuition, clairvoyance, and mental clarity (or lack thereof).

You are about to experiment with opening your third eye and exploring the space of your vision center. Do you have an impression of a
dominant color or colors as you approach this energy center?

Remove your finger from the third eye area and feel yourself looking out through something like a window, a telescope, or a viewfinder.
With your ordinary eyes closed, test how much you can see when you
look out through this porthole, and notice the *way* you see. If everything
is grainy and dark to begin with, relax and continue to look. Pictures
may begin to emerge. You may find yourself looking out into the external environment, or into your immediate psychic space, or into a dra-
matically different scene.

Now feel yourself looking *inward*, into the space behind the window. What is the scene inside? Is it cramped or spacious? Is it cluttered
or pleasantly arranged? Is there something that could be done in this
area to improve your vision?

Practice looking out through the porthole of the third eye again.

As you move your attention from "inside" to "outside," is there a
life-form — bird or animal or other — that appears to you?

Draw a symbol for the vision center on your Living Totem Pole.

Seventh Chakra: Crown Center

You are now prepared for the final, and highest, ascent. With your
awareness, you travel up to the top of your head, and beyond your physical head, into the space of the crown center. You are entering a realm of
light and openness to Spirit.

Do you feel the light? Do you have the impression of colors?

You are flowing gently into a vast and generous space filled with
light.

Let your awareness float upward. You are beginning to perceive living symbols that embody your connections to the spiritual world and to
the spiritual traditions that humans have honored across millennia. You
may encounter birds and animals, humans and angels, gods and gurus.

What is the life-form or living symbol that emerges most strongly? Explore the nature of your connection with this entity.

Bring some of its energy with you as you gather up your impressions and embark on the return journey.

Draw the living symbol you found at the crown center at the top of your Living Totem Pole.

Return Journey

It is time to return from your journey through the energy centers. Let your awareness move gently down to your heart. As you move your awareness to the heart center, feel your heart filling with light that is streaming down from your crown center.

Feel earth energy streaming up from the soles of your feet, through your root center, up through the lower centers to your heart.

Let the energy of earth and the radiance of light join at your heart. As the twin streams of energy come together at the heart, you may receive an image of their sacred union.

Now you are ready to work with the insights you have been given, which are to follow the natural paths of your energy and bring empowerment and healing, as well as the wisdom of the heart.

Partner Work with Your Energy Map

A partner may be able to help you move decisively toward healing and balancing by "talking" you through the challenges — and powers — that are depicted in your energy map. Here's a simple example from a workshop I led in Canada. From her diagnostic journey, Rosemary reported:

> Snakes are coiled around my throat, constricting it painfully. Under their bodies, a flower is struggling to survive. The color inside is sickly white. I want these snakes off me; they are choking me.

I asked Rosemary to stay with this vision, though it made her extremely uncomfortable. I asked her if she could remember back to any point in her earlier life where she had felt the same sense of being choked. She was initially unable to speak. I asked what she needed to do to remove what was choking her.

"I guess I need to say something," she finally croaked.

"Where in your body does that need to come from?"

"From the heart."

"What do you need to say?"

"I guess the word is —" she faltered and became inaudible.

"Yes?"

"I guess the word is *love*." Tears were streaming down her cheeks.

"Can you say that louder?"

"I don't think so." She dabbed at her nose and eyes with a bunch of tissues.

"Suppose we make a song out of it, and sing it together. I'll sing if you will. What's wrong with that?"

"I can't do it." She was shaking.

"Sure you can. Here we go," I told her.

Love, Love
Love, Love
Love brings my world
into Being.

The song came welling up out of an experience of deep spontaneous healing that had come to me many years before. It took a couple of rounds before Rosemary was able to join in fully. When we were done singing, she touched her throat, gently feeling her way around her neck. Her eyes widened. "They've gone," she said. She went to her heart center to find what she needed to say, and when she spoke from the heart, her throat center opened. To deal with a challenge at one energy center, she had to go to another and draw strength from that.

Healing Journey through Your Personal Energy Map

Your personal energy map can be used to go far beyond discussion or meditation. It can be your road map for a profound journey of release and empowerment.

The *weak spots* in your energy map are of the greatest interest in preparing for the healing journey.

Suppose you find only a little egg in the root center. This may be an invitation to let something hatch — to connect with (or create) a broader community, to do work in the world, to heal a whole family.

A man in one of my workshops found a *huge* amount of potential energy in his solar plexus (he thought it looked like a hydroelectric plant), but the only life-form in the scene was a mouse. He decided he needed to go to another energy center, where he found a braver animal. He took its courage and tracking skills with him on a return journey to the solar plexus to tap into his unused reserves of personal power.

Maybe you find you are choked or blocked or constricted at the throat center — a common condition in our society. It will be very interesting to journey back to examine exactly what has been silencing your voice. One woman found that what was choking her was a literal choker — a powder blue, lacy choker woven and tightened by generations of women in her family who had accepted subservient roles. Another journeyer found that her ex was holding the other end of the rope around her neck. A third discovered that she had lost her voice because there was something blocking the path from her heart to her mouth. Each of these travelers succeeded in opening their throat centers during their healing journeys, with the help of allies located in and recruited from other power places in their energy systems.

You could find that your second chakra is dry and sterile instead of moist and juicy and flowing. This is an invitation to find and open the sluices of creative passion and inundate and revive the dormant fields.

How do we respond to such invitations?

By making a second and deeper journey. Here's how to do this with a partner as a therapeutic exercise in conscious, shared dreaming.

EXERCISE

Shared Dreaming for Healing via the Energy Map

Sit with your partner and take turns sharing your personal energy charts. Help each other to identify the principal areas of challenge or blockage and the places where you feel the most power.

You are getting ready to support each other on a journey of healing and balancing — actually *two* journeys, since you will take turns playing dreamer and tracker.

After your sharing, decide who will go first. We'll call that person the dreamer. Her energy map will guide the first of the healing journeys. The itinerary might be as follows:

- Go to the place in your energy chart where you feel the most power. It might be any of the chakras; there is no right or wrong one. If you found equal power in two or more chakras, pick your point of departure; every journey has to start somewhere.

- During the drumming, go to that energy center and collect your power. More likely than not, this will be an animal guardian — the dragon at your root center, the eagle at your third eye, the wild horses at your solar plexus, or whatever.

- Travel with that power to the places of weakness or blockage. You may go directly there, or you may choose to journey through the energy centers again until you come to that place of challenge. Let's say you found dragon power in your root center but feel choked and constricted at your throat center. You could fly directly to your throat center with that dragon fire and see whether you can use it to burn away that noose. Or you could travel up through the second, third, and fourth chakras, raising the dragon stage by stage, gathering further juice and heart wisdom. The second approach appeals to me more, and is likely to work better, because in it you establish an energy flow that can move harmoniously through your whole system.

- The tracker's role in this journey is to support the dreamer in any way that is helpful. The dreamer may want the tracker to play an activist role — in which case the tracker may enlist the support of her own power allies (those discovered during the diagnostic journey and/or others that may be available).

- After the journey, dreamer and tracker share their travel reports, and the dreamer is goaded to come up with an action plan to honor the experience. For example, if your challenge involved the throat center, now is the time to stand up and sing or shout.

From Diagnostic to Healing Journeys: Travel Reports

Here are travel reports from participants in my workshops describing the use of the energy map from the diagnostic journey to embark on a deeper journey for healing.

Healed by the Bear and the Shaman's Penis-Staff

A Chicago man found several areas of concern in his diagnostic journey. At his second chakra, everything seemed cold, rigid, and lifeless: a frozen apple atop a pile of green stones in space like a freezer. At his throat center, he found complicated gates and barriers. At his third eye, he felt like his eyelids had been glued shut.

But in the course of his initial journey, he also found an ally: a black bear standing in a shaft of bright light in a "humming, energized" space at his solar plexus. And in the space of his crown center, he found an enigmatic *potential* ally: "an immense African mask three or four times my height."

In discussion, he decided to begin his healing journey by going to the place of the bear, his solar plexus. Soon after the drumming began, he found himself traveling with the bear. It was a vivid experience in which the bear took the initiative. "The bear reached with his paw and somehow removed my closed eyelids so that I could see better. Then he smeared yellow-gray mud on my third eye, and it opened. He brought me to my throat center, where I had found the gates that could not be opened. The bear just pulled them apart like taffy!"

The bear brought him up to the crown center, where the huge African mask now swung open like a door. "I was greeted by a figure wearing a feather and bird headdress or mask. He had a long staff with feathers along its length at intervals, and at the top was an enormous red gem. He used this gem to heal my sex center. As the glowing red tip of his staff touched the green stones in my second chakra, the cold room became warm and vibrant with life, and the apple became juicy."

After this experience, the Chicago man reported major break-throughs in office communications and writing — and a big improvement in his sex life.

Healing with Sunflower Light and the Bird Dancer

In her diagnostic journey, Diane found two problem areas: a black, cavernous, uninhabitable space at her second chakra, and a "tiny, skinny chink" of an opening at her throat center. She also found a place of power, in the joyful "sunflower light" of her crown center. In this realm, she was delighted to find a magical world of Faerie, and spiritual helpers from among both her own Celtic ancestors and those of the First Peoples of northeast America, where she lived. A bird dancer came whirling and spinning.

With the dancer's help — and that of a magical bluebird that appeared — she was able to return to her constricted throat center during the initial journey. The bird dancer "kept singing and dancing and spinning and opening the space wider and wider until it was fully capable of holding him and all his regalia and voice in that space."

But she still had to deal with that black void in her sex-creative center. She agreed with her partner that she would start out by returning to her crown center and gathering the "sunflower light," and then would try to flood the dark space with that radiant energy. "I was taking the joy and the yellow sunflower light to that area to help fill the void and to make it habitable and fertile. My partner was bringing glowing light energy of her own. The bird dancer came through and helped me dance the joy into being."

She came back feeling restored and renewed, ready for life.

Lending a Lovable Mutt

In the diagnostic journey, Linda experienced a particularly severe blockage in her throat center. As her plan for a healing journey, she decided to gather light from the crown center and try to clean out the blockage with the power of this light.

Her partner, Jane, felt particularly strong in her heart center. In the initial meditation, she had found a "lovable mutt" in her heart space, and she felt that he offered the gift of unconditional love.

Linda's efforts to bring light did not prosper. She felt stuck and increasingly desperate.

Jane devoted herself to trying to send her "lovable mutt" to Linda's throat center to clear the blockage. She felt the transfer was effective. She saw the dog going to work, trying to pull something out of Linda's throat. The dog took over completely. Then Jane's imagery stopped. "I almost went to sleep."

Meanwhile, in her frustration, Linda was surprised to see something being pushed into her field of vision, from the right side, where Jane was lying next to her. This was very clearly an insert, not a pop-up from her personal unconscious. She was surprised to see that a long-stemmed red rose was being pushed toward her. She recognized that someone was giving her a gift. As she watched, the head of the rose opened and a dog emerged — a "lovable mutt." It licked her neck. Then the dog clamped his jaws around her throat and started pulling. Something like a large ball of "gunk" started to tear loose. But it was slow to come out. As the drum sounded the recall, Linda was terrified that she would be left with the gunk in her throat and the dog clamped to her windpipe. With a last tremendous tug, the dog ripped out a big, glutinous mass — and Linda found that her throat was clear.

Energy Maps for Conscious Living

When you have made your energy map from your personal journey, you'll find you have a clearer understanding of what needs to be fed and nourished in your body and your life. The lion will require you to find your courage and speak your truth; the deer will want you to graze; the snake will invite you to shed the skin of old habits and dead history. You'll have new lenses for conscious living as you find yourself asking, regarding any issue: Does this involve my power center, or my heart? Is this a root issue, or a sex thing?

This kind of awareness can be helpful in everyday interactions with other people. The day after leading a chakra workshop, I had a confrontation with a very large and very angry young man in the street. My first reflex was to respond from my solar plexus. But I was able to take a deep breath, scan my own energy response, and make the choice to respond from the root center (community survival) and then from the heart center. As I consciously switched the movement of my energy, a nasty conflict was defused, the young man's anger dissolved, and we parted on good terms.

10

Low-Maintenance Plan
for Psychic Good Health

Good fences make good neighbors.

— ROBERT FROST

To live consciously, we need to recognize that we walk every day in a mind-field of overlapping thoughts and energies. We need a daily practice that supports psychic as well as physical health and well-being. We need to be able to recognize signs of psychic disturbance and energy imbalance, and to be ready to offer a quick and effective response.

On an everyday basis, psychic good health depends, first and last, on exercising common sense, staying grounded, maintaining good boundaries — and keeping a sense of humor. The fundamentals are very simple:

Ground yourself. Spend time in nature. Stay connected with the elemental powers of earth and air, fire and water. Walk in the park, go swimming or jogging, sit with the sun or with a tree.

Invoke blessing and protection. Know that even when you feel most alone, help is always available. I start every day by invoking the Gatekeeper, that power that opens and closes our doors in life. Your invocation might encompass all the powers that support your life, including the God or Goddess you can talk to. Like Native Americans, I like to invoke the sacred powers by giving thanks for both the blessings and the challenges of this lifetime.

Check your boundaries. Be careful what you invite into your space, in every sense. Monitor your thoughts and feelings. You want to be able to distinguish what belongs to you and what does not. If you find an image or obscure life memory surfacing for no apparent reason, or a sudden shift in your feelings or energy level, look to see whether you are picking it up from something else. If you are experiencing a sudden dip or energy drain, scout out the reason why. Sudden loss of energy may be a sign that something has breached your energy field and that your aura is in need of repair.

Choose the day. At every turning, *choose* where you put the energy of your attention. Energy flows where attention goes. Do something every day to connect with the center of your Self and to act from your personal truth as you have now learned to define it. Live as if you mean it, in the knowledge that the only time is now. Don't lose yourself in guilt over the past or fear about the future.

Lighten up! I mean this in twin senses — call on light, and find a reason to laugh, despite everything. Among traditional Iroquois, when someone is sick or depressed, the most high-energy, humorous people in the community are summoned to the sickroom to make lots of happy noise and laughter. The understanding is that the spirits who bring illness and misfortune can't stand people having good clean fun and will leave in disgust. Sir Thomas More offered a parallel insight: "The devil, that proud sprite, cannot bear to be mocked." Do something several times a day that makes you *laugh*.

Strengthening and Sealing the Energy Body

We go through life in more than one body. Around our physical body is an energy field that is our first line of interface with the world around us. Through this energy body, we pick up the thoughts and feelings of people around us, as well as collective energies and thought forms. Just as we need to take care of the health of our physical bodies, we need to tend to the well-being of our energy bodies.

Here is a daily meditation for strengthening and shielding the energy field. Through this simple daily meditation, we can strengthen and tone our energy bodies and set healthy psychic boundaries.

EXERCISE

The Light around You

1. Growing the Energy Tree

Start by standing or sitting with your back straight. Pay attention to the flow of your breath. As you breathe in through your nose, make it your intention to breathe in clean, fresh energy. As you exhale through your mouth, feel yourself beginning to release any negative or heavy energy — and stress or anxiety or fear — that is with you.

Now let your awareness move to the soles of your feet. Feel yourself reaching down, with your awareness, through the soles of your feet, down into the earth. You are reaching down deep, as the roots of a tree go deep and spread wide. You begin to feel the warmth and moisture of Mother Earth, and you feel yourself becoming rooted and centered in the earth.

Now you are ready to let the energy of earth rise up gently into your body…up through your feet, and up through your legs, stirring and working in you. It is rising up through your root center, and your second chakra…and up through your solar plexus…and you are stronger with each breath. And the earth energy rises to your heart…and up through your throat center, loosening any blockage or constriction. And up to your third eye…and up to the crown of your head…and the earth energy rises above the top of your head and streams down around you like a soft mist, returning to its source.

Take some deep breaths and let the whole cycle renew and deepen in you…

As you breathe in, let the earth energy rise through all of your body …As you exhale, let it gently return to its source…

And as you breathe out, feel the earth energy flushing away any heavy or dead energies that are with you. Let those heavy energies be absorbed into the earth…

You are already stronger and lighter, and you rise like a tree, between earth and sky, rooted in the earth, grounded and centered, joined in a cycle of endlessly renewing energy…

2. Bringing Down the Light

Now let your awareness float up to the top of your head…and above your head…

You are becoming aware of the immense energy of a light, brighter and stronger than the sun, that is streaming down to you from All That Is…

And you are ready to open yourself at the crown of your head to the infinite, invincible power of light. You are opening like a flower, like a chalice…and the light streams down, shining, through the crown of your head…and flows down, shining, to your third eye…and streams down, shining, through your throat center…and washes down through your solar plexus. It streams down, shining, through the lower centers of your body…and washes down through your legs…and moves beneath you and around you. And it streams up your spine…and surges down through the crown of your head again…

You are within the light. You are surrounded by light. You are in a place where you are loved and protected.

As you breathe in, drink the light. Feel the light moving through every fiber and particle of your being. Feel the light moving over the surface of your skin and glowing beyond your skin, so you stand robed in a radiant aura of light.

Feel the light growing stronger and brighter at your heart. Drink the light, and let it pool at your heart.

Now open your heart — and your lungs — and make the sound that wants to come from your heart.

3. Scanning the Surface of Your Energy Body

In the light that is with you, you can now perceive and scan the surface of your energy field. It may appear to you as a web of energy filaments.

Now you allow your awareness to sense whether there are any rips or holes or weaknesses in your energy web. These are places where you may be vulnerable to energy intrusion.

If you find places where your energy web needs repairing, you may now call in extra light to make the needed repairs. If your energy web appears intact, the next phase of the meditation will still bring you greater strength, which will help you to cope with all of life's challenges.

4. Igniting Your Inner Sun

You stand with the light, and you are rooted in the earth.

Let your awareness move back down to your feet, and feel again how you are rooted in the earth. Let the earth energy continue to rise through your body, strengthening and cleansing. Let the earth energy rise to your solar plexus — above and around your belly button — and hold it there.

Now feel the light continuing to stream through you in great abundance. Let the light pour down through your heart to your solar plexus, where it meets the rising stream of earth energy. As the energy of light and the energy of earth meet in your solar plexus, you feel the immense power of warmth and light growing inside you. It grows stronger and brighter until it blazes like an inner sun.

5. Repairing and Renewing Your Energy Web

Take the power that is now with you and mend or strengthen the surface of your energy field. You may see yourself stitching separated fibers together…or smoothing out places that are rumpled…or brightening a dark or dull patch…or washing away spots with cleansing light…

Let the light that is with you fill and charge the whole of your energy field.

6. Choosing the Shape of Your Energy Body

Now study the shape of the energy field around you. How does your energy body seem to you today? Your energy body may be in its default mode — an egg-shaped cocoon or bubble. But its shape, color, and decoration can be changed by your intention.

7. Setting Your Energy Boundaries

As you start your day, you'll also want to consider where you should set your energy boundaries. You'll want to pull them in tight and close if you are likely to be exposed to confused and conflictive feelings and energies.

As part of your self-scanning, check to see whether you have any unwanted cords of psychic connection that may be draining or confusing your energy. The Hawaiian kahunas say we are linked by *aka* cords — cords of subtle energetic material that link us to anyone who has ever touched our lives — unless they are cut. Where we have a robust, healthy relationship with a lover, friend, or colleague, these cords may resemble thick umbilicals, pumping juice both ways in a happy exchange. But when the energy flow is imbalanced, or the cord is a legacy from a relationship that turned bad, these psychic cords become a major problem. They are a principal conduit for energy theft, and we need to learn how and when to shut them off. If you feel this is a problem, here's a gentle but highly effective way to resolve it:

Sense where on your energy body you may have an attachment to someone who is draining your energy. Picture that attachment as an electrical extension cord plugged into a location in your energy anatomy. Common "outlets" are the solar plexus and the second chakra.

Now picture yourself unplugging that energy cord, pulling it out as you might pull a plug out of an outlet in the wall.

Follow up by visualizing yourself restoring and strengthening your energy boundaries over the place of the former attachment. Now go take a vigorous shower or a walk outside.

11

Finding and Living Your Essential Story

It is the easiest thing in the world to tell a story — and the hardest to be a fine storyteller.... To be a good storyteller one must be gloriously alive.

— RUTH SAWYER, *The Way of the Storyteller*

We live by stories. Our first and best teachers, in our lives and in the evolution of our kind, instruct and inspire by telling stories. Story is our shortest route to the meaning of things, and our easiest way to remember and carry the meaning we discover. A good story lives inside and outside time and gives us keys to a world of truth beyond the world of fact.

Consciously or unconsciously, our lives are directed by stories. If we are not aware that we are living a story, it's likely we are stuck inside a narrow and constricted one, a story bound tight around us by other people's definitions and expectations. When we reach, consciously, for a bigger life story, we put ourselves in touch with tremendous sources of healing, creativity, and courage.

How do we find the bigger story in our lives? The answer is easier than we might think. The First Peoples of my native Australia say that the big stories are hunting the right people to tell them. All we need do is put ourselves in places where we can be found.

J. M. G. Clézio dedicated his Nobel Prize for Literature to Elvira, a storyteller of the rain forest of Darién, in Central America, a woman who roamed from house to house spinning magic words in return for a meal or a drink. In his acceptance speech, Le Clézio painted a vivid word-picture of Elvira: "I quickly realized that she was a great artist, in the best sense of the term. The timbre of her voice, the rhythm of her hands tapping against her chest, against her heavy necklaces of silver coins, and above all the air of possession which illuminated her face and her gaze, a sort of measured, rhythmic trance, exerted a power over all those who were present. To the simple framework of her myths…she added her own story, her life of wandering, her loves, the betrayals and suffering, the intense joy of carnal love, the sting of jealousy, her fear of growing old, of dying. She was poetry in action, ancient theatre, and the most contemporary of novels all at the same time."

Is it too late to hope we can bring back storytelling in our modern urban headphonelands? I think not. And as we practice telling our dreams and the stories of our life experiences simply and vividly, we become bards and griots and storytellers without labor. The first step in the Lightning Dreamwork game, introduced earlier in the book, requires us to encourage whoever is ready to tell a dream (or, for that matter, any life experience) to tell it simply and clearly, without background or analysis or interruption or reading from notes. We give undivided attention for the duration of the telling and require the teller not to miss the opportunity to claim her audience.

On the popular overnight radio show *Coast to Coast AM*, George Noory asked me to demonstrate the Lightning Dreamwork process. I asked him to tell me a story from any part of his life. George thought for a moment and came up with a tale of how he felt so pressed for time that one night he consumed a lavish meal in a fancy restaurant in ten minutes flat, and found himself reddening with embarrassment as the others at the table stared at his empty plate. We proceeded to discuss the moral in the tale, which could make any of us think about where in our lives we are not allowing ourselves to relax and let things flow (and let the stomach gently receive the gifts of the table). I found myself seized by the theme and so engrossed in George's telling that I had to take off my wristwatch in the midst of the show to give myself a sense of physical release from the entrapment of clock time.

Wake Up and Smell the Stories

"I heard something scratching at my door in the middle of the night," the young man in the front row began. "When I opened the door, I found my dead cat, the one that died a couple of months ago. Then I noticed my house had four stories, which is a couple more than it ordinarily has. I was wondering what was going on in those extra stories up top. Then I heard my dad's voice. He was calling to me, 'Hurry up! You don't want to miss the music!'"

"How did you feel when you woke up?" (It's the first question to ask about any dream.)

"Kind of nervous. My dad passed last spring, and I didn't know what he meant."

"Have you had any previous contact with your father since he passed?"

"Oh sure. I feel like he's been dealing with a lot of stuff, and I've been helping."

"How did your father sound, when he spoke about the music?"

"He sounded really happy. Like something happy was going on."

"If it were my dream," I said carefully, "I might think: My father's discovered something really good, and he wants to share it with me. Maybe he wants to show me that he's found his way, in his new life. If it were my dream, I might want to see if I could have a proper conversation with my dad. I'd want to know the rest of our story. Those extra levels to the house give me the sense of space and possibility. I might want to light a candle for Dad and put out something personal pertaining to him, like a photo, and maybe something to eat or drink that he would enjoy, and see whether I could just start up a dialogue. Could you give that a try?"

"Sure," the young man replied, nodding. "I like the idea of getting the rest of the story."

I looked around the group of eager faces at a local community center. "Would anyone else like to share a dream?" A few hands went up.

This was a group of newbies. For many of them, this was the first time they had told a story in front of a group. For some of them, this was the first time they had talked about a dream in their whole adult lives.

"I dreamed I went to this very pricey restaurant," an older woman began. "I started sipping a glass of wine, and the glass broke in my teeth and the shards of glass were inside my mouth, stabbing me. I was trying to tell people what had happened, and that I needed help, but they wouldn't believe me, even though there was blood everywhere."

"How did you feel when you woke up?"

"I couldn't understand why they wouldn't believe me."

"Yes, and how did you *feel* about that?"

"It's hard to say. Disturbed."

"But you didn't feel frightened, for example? Or disgusted?"

"Nothing that strong."

"Well, that's interesting. That sets a little distance. Sometimes it's revealing that we don't have strong feelings about a dream. Reality check — could you go to a restaurant like that in the future?"

"Sure."

"Is it possible this could involve an occasion, maybe with family, when there is some conflict brewing and it's difficult to say your piece?"

"That's entirely possible."

"If it were my dream," I said, pursuing the point, "I'd think about the broken glass in terms of emotional conflicts. I'd think about my need to express myself in such a way that others can hear me and believe me, whatever I need to get out."

This resonated deeply with the dreamer. After more discussion, I asked her for an action plan. She said she would start by keeping a journal, in that way getting practice in saying what she needed to say. "Can you come up with a one-liner that moves in that direction?" She produced one right away: "I'm going to tell my story."

This threw my mind back to something I had seen that morning in my local paper, at the bottom of the local news page. It was an ad for coffee. Across a landscape of green mountains scrolled the following text: *I realized today's the day I will tell my story.*

The ability to tell our story — and in doing so, choose the stories we are living — is not only a creative gift; it is also a vital survival tool.

Another woman in the group, slightly diffident, began to talk about a recurring dream from which she was always relieved to wake up. "I have a baby, maybe eighteen months old, and I'm supposed to take care of her. I want to get away because I don't know who she is."

When I asked some questions, she added, "The baby is fine. I'm the one who's not fine."

"If it were my dream, I might wonder whether what I was running from was actually a part of myself. I might want to sit down quietly, at the right time, and take a closer look at that very young child and see whether she is a very young part of me that separated out for some reason but is now ready to bring her joy and energy into my life."

This struck a chord. She was willing to give it a try. Through our dream stories, we sometimes find that a missing part of us is calling to us, seeking a way to gain entry to our lives, to make us stronger and more whole.

Six Universal Stories

In a dream I recorded in my 2003 journal, I am encouraging people to open their mouths and their throat centers and to let their stories out. I tell them firmly that they mustn't eat or try to do anything else that would interfere with their vocal passages at the same time. I suggest they can take one of six universal stories and retell it as the pattern of their own lives, changing details — and outcomes — as they find appropriate.

I tell them there will be a special reward for successful storytellers: a reserved parking space in a rooftop lot. Reserved spaces are defined by green lines. There are also green signs identifying the people for whom spaces are reserved. A larger sign announces that many more spaces will be available when the right storytellers appear.

I woke in high excitement with the strong desire to manifest this dream.

I was not sure then — nor am I today — what the "six universal stories" are, but I am inspired to offer six that resonate with me, drawing from various sources.

Killing the Demon of Repetition

In an earlier chapter, we explored the power of naming personal demons. As demons go, one of the scariest (because it's most likely to turn
up any day, recognized or not) is one of the most unlikely: the parrot.
Why? Well, if you think about what you most associate with parrots,
other than bright colors and finger nipping, you may have the answer.
But let's hear the story before the commentary.

The story comes from Persia, and it is about a hero on a quest. The
hero's name, some say, is Hatim Tai, and he is a prince. The prince is
summoned by his king and given an interesting assignment. He is to
search for a mysterious castle known as the Bath Badgerd — the Castle
of Nonexistence — and find out what is there. He sets out on a long
journey on which he must battle with monsters and face every kind of
hardship. Everyone he meets gives him a reason to abandon his mission.
People are unanimous on one point: no traveler who reached the castle
has ever returned.

The hero is not dismayed. At last he comes to a round, domed
building that must be part of the Bath Badgerd. He is greeted by a hairdresser who is carrying a mirror, and is invited to wash off the dust of
the journey in a beautiful pool. As soon as he enters the water, there is
the roar of thunder and the water level starts to rise. He thrashes about
in the pool but can't escape. The water is rushing him up toward the
ceiling. He's going to drown. But with his last breath, he cries out for
divine help and grabs for the keystone above him.

This changes everything. There is more rolling thunder and the hero
is transported, quick as thought, to the middle of a hot desert. His or-
deals begin again, and it requires much wandering on dragging, bloody
feet before he comes to a beautiful garden. He is now at the very heart of
the Bath Badgerd and about to face the greatest of his challenges.

In the midst of the garden is a circle of stone statues. They are very
lifelike; each figure looks like a person frozen in the midst of a cry or a
violent motion of the upper body. At the center of this circle is a parrot
in a cage. Under the unfriendly eye of the parrot, there is a golden bow,
and a golden arrow chained to the cage.

A voice from above explains the scene. "What you are seeking is here, but you won't live to see it. The stone men are those who tried before you and became petrified. The treasure of this place is a diamond beyond price that was hidden here by Gayomart, the First Man. In order to claim it, you must kill the parrot. The bow and arrow are your weapons. You have three chances to shoot the parrot. If you fail, you will be petrified."

How hard can it be to shoot a parrot at close range? The state of the stone men is not encouraging, but the hero takes up the bow and lets fly. The arrow flies wide, the parrot cackles — and the prince is turned to stone from his feet to his crotch. Before shooting the second arrow, he takes extra care with his aim. He misses again and is turned to stone up to the base of his heart. Now he remembers how he escaped being drowned in the flood, by invoking a higher power. He shuts his eyes, calls on his God, and fires without calculation. The arrow finds its mark. With a boom of thunder, the parrot vanishes. In its place appears the great jewel of the First Man, the diamond of the greater Self, and the petrified men are released from the spell.

Marie-Louise von Franz found this old Persian fairy story to be a parable of "individuation" — the Jungian term for the process by which an individual advances toward the embodiment of his or her true Self.[18] All of the symbols are rich in meaning: the round building, the barber (or hairdresser), the mirror, the fast-rising waters. But let's stay with the demon. Of all the adversaries and obstacles the hero must overcome on his journey to find the jewel beyond price, the most formidable is a parrot in a cage.

We can now answer the question "Why?": because we can never get to the greater Self by copying other people or by repeating ourselves. The parrot is famous for doing both: for imitating others and for endless repetition. When we fail to kill the demon of imitation and repetition in our lives, we consign ourselves to the petrified human forest.

Waking the Sleeping King

In one of Madame d'Aulnoy's classic fairy stories, "The Blue Bird," an abused princess survives incredible trials and transformations. Disguised as a beggar girl, she at last manages to gain access to the Echo

Chamber in the castle of King Charming, who loves her as she loves him but believes her lost. What is said in the Echo Chamber can be heard distinctly in the royal bedchamber above. The princess wails her story of love and loss, assuming it will awaken the king to the fact that she is alive and available and recall him to the pledges they exchanged.

But night after night, the king fails to hear. The princess has used up nearly all of the magic a good witch gave her — which has enabled her to buy entry to the Echo Chamber — before she learns that the king does not hear her because he takes a sleeping potion every night. She manages to bribe a page to withhold the sleeping potion. Awake in the night, the king hears her love pleas and goes in search of her, and they are united.

This is a much more relevant story for our times than the theme of the sleeping princess. Here the woman has to wake up the man, as is much more often the case. How many "sleeping kings" do we know? How many forms do their "sleeping potions " take? Whenever you run into a guy who has lost touch with his dreams, who may even say, "I don't dream," remember you may be dealing with a sleeping king, and *you* may be called on to play the role of the awakener.

The very adult message in this story made me want to know more about the author. Where did her clarity of perception, among all the fantasy and finery (and raw horror too), come from? The story of the author of "The Blue Bird" is fascinating and takes us into the raw depths of lived experience from which the pre-Disney and pre-Victorian fairy tales come — in this case, not from peasant folklore but from the no less brutal life dramas of France's real-life princesses.

At age fifteen, Marie-Catherine Le Jumel de Barneville was kidnapped from a convent school and raped under the pretext of an arranged marriage — the polite name for an arrangement by which her father sold her to a rich and depraved aristocrat three times her age. The baron d'Aulnoy was odious, a heavy drinker and gambler with unpleasant sexual penchants. Three years into the marriage, it looked like Marie-Catherine had found a way out of her cage when her husband was arrested on charges of high treason against the king. However, under torture two of the accusers confessed that they had invented the treason charges because they were Marie-Catherine's secret lovers. The baroness had to flee to Spain, where she restored herself to royal favor — over many years — by functioning as a secret agent for the French. We derive the term *fairy tale* from this extraordinary survivor, Marie-Catherine d'Aulnoy. She titled her first collection, published in 1697, *Les contes des fées*. She spun her tales for adults, rather than children, in her seventeenth-century salon, in fashionable colloquial style, as reflected in the subtitle of her second collection, *Les fées à la mode*. Hers is a true-life story of spinning soiled hay into gold.[19]

Long Journey to Find the Treasure in the Backyard

This ever-recurring story is the theme of Paulo Coelho's novel *The Alchemist*. In this version, a shepherd boy named Santiago follows a dream — and his heart's desire — from his homeland in Spain to the Egyptian desert in search of a treasure he dreamed would be buried under the pyramids. He finds guidance in his journey in words of wisdom and in hard lessons that expand his journey into years. He surmounts the obstacles, learns lessons of the heart and soul, and discovers in a moment of supreme disappointment that his treasure is not where he expected it to be. At that defining moment, a stranger shares his own dream of treasure, and the boy — now a man — recognizes his original homeland in the stranger's dream. He returns to Spain to find the treasure in the place where he started.

The theme reverberates throughout world literature. In *The Book of the Thousand Nights and One Night*, a once-wealthy man in Baghdad who loses all that he owns dreams that a man tells him: "Your fortune is in Cairo; go there and seek it." So he sets out for Cairo, is beaten, robbed, and thrown in jail. Despairing, he tells what he now believes to be a cruelly deceptive dream to his jailer, who laughs and reports, "A man has come to me three times in a dream and has described a house in Baghdad where a vast amount of money is supposedly buried beneath a fountain in the garden. He told me to go there and take it, but I stayed here. You, however, have foolishly journeyed from place to place on the faith of a dream that was nothing more than a meaningless hallucination." The prisoner recognizes the house in the jailer's dream as his own, but is smart enough not to reveal this. Feeling sorry for the poor fool, the jailer frees the traveler, who returns home and digs up the treasure that was waiting for him in his own backyard.

We may have to journey far and meet many challenges before we are able to open our hearts and discover the treasure that was always there. As T. S. Eliot wrote in "Little Gidding":

> We shall not cease from exploration.
> And the end of all our exploring
> Will be to arrive where we started
> And know the place for the first time.

And that changes everything.

Becoming the Big O

Do you remember *The Missing Piece Meets the Big O*, Shel Silverstein's delightful parable for kids of all ages? My youngest daughter told me when she was a junior in college that it was *the* best story we read together when she was very young.

With the aid of wickedly simple line drawings, we follow the adventures and travails of what looks like a slice of pie. She's trying to find a hole she can fit and tries various orifices that turn up, in characters she encounters.

Eventually she finds what seems to be Mr. Right. He looks like a pie missing a wedge, and the missing piece slips into the hole and the fit seems perfect. But then the missing piece starts to grow, and grow, until her host complains, "I didn't know you were going to grow." The missing piece is ejected, and the character with the hole lumbers away, caterwauling, "I'm looking for my missin' piece, one that won't increase."

We come to the denouement of the story. A character comes along who is different from the rest. He is not one of the hungry ones, or the shy ones, and there is no hole in him at all. He is the Big O. The missing piece would love to join him, but there is no place where she could fit. Can't she at least travel on his back as he rolls along? Nope, the Big O is not going to carry her. "But perhaps you can roll by yourself," he tells her. She is incredulous. How can she roll on her sharp corners? "Corners wear off," says the Big O, "and shapes change."

The missing piece just sits for a long time, despondent, when the Big O rolls away. Then very slowly she hauls herself up and flops over. And does it again. And her edges start to wear off, and she is bumping instead of flopping, then bouncing instead of bumping, until at last she is *rolling*.

There is a terrific lesson in this simple tale, and for me it's all about soul and soul making. All those creatures with holes in them evoke the loss of soul any one of us is likely to suffer in the course of a life via pain or shame or disappointment. The hunger this creates can't be filled authentically by something that is not our own.

Nor can we find our way in life by trying to fill a gap in another person, or a niche in a social or work environment, or by just sitting around waiting for something to happen. We need to pick ourselves up and — unaccustomed though this may be — start moving according to our own inner lights. And let the road smooth out our sharp edges and put curves in our linear thinking.

Instead of trying to fit a hole, we want to become whole. To be pals with the Big O, you have to become your own Big O.

A Mirror for the Sun Goddess

Shamed and abused by the people around you — especially the men in your life — you withdraw into a dark and hidden place and your light is gone from the world.

In your absence, the world is sad and wan. Nothing grows or flourishes.

The people you left are desperate to bring you back. They call to you in your place of solitude, offering promises and gifts. You won't listen, until one day you hear laughter. It's not the canned laughter of a prime-time sitcom. This is the laughter that surges from life, rich and earthy and organic, the laughter that comes from the belly.

It tickles you and tempts you. Curious, you start climbing up from your dark place to see what's going on. Suddenly there is light before you, and in that light you see a beautiful, radiant figure. And rapture seizes your heart. You want to embrace this beautiful being, because surely this is the beloved of your soul, the one you have always hoped for.

As you reach for your beloved, the figure withdraws. You follow, moving ever upward, out of the cold underworld to which you exiled yourself. Now strong hands seize you, drawing you into the world above, the world you abandoned.

Now you see that the one who captured your heart is your own reflected self shining from a mirror. The deception was not deceit, simply a way to show you your true Self.

You are received with honor back in the world, and light and growth return to it, thanks to you.

This is my simple retelling of one of the great stories of soul healing as a return to the greater Self. I have borrowed it from Japan, where the abused woman who abandons the world is no less that Amaterasu, the sun goddess. Visit her temples, and you'll see mirrors hanging everywhere, a reminder of her ordeal and her homecoming. When we locate the drama of Amaterasu in our own lives, we begin to make a mirror to reflect the radiance of the larger Self that can help to bring us, and those we love, up from the dark places.

The Forgetful Envoy

You are sent from your homeland on an important mission, to rescue something beyond price. You understand the enormous risks of this assignment, and you freely choose to fulfill it. On leaving your homeland, you are honored and mourned, because you are dying, for a time, to those who love you and know you best.

The conditions of your assignment require you to put on the clothes and habits of the country where you will operate. You must fit in with those around you and follow their ways. This is hard for you in the beginning, because people here live as if there were nothing beyond their world of getting and spending. Their pleasures are tawdry and their drugs numb the mind, but you are required to pass for one of them, so you do as they do.

In the miasmic conditions of this plane, you start to forget why you came here. Your memory of your homeland, of its achingly beautiful music and its true communion of souls, seems like a fantastic dream and is starting to fade away. You let those around you in your new country tell you what life is about, and you act in accordance with their valuation of things.

You join them in snickering at dreamers who rant of other worlds.

Then one night there is a knock at your door. You open it and feel a strange wind, like the beating of giant wings. The person framed in the doorway is strangely familiar. When he speaks, his words leap to your heart. "I come from my father's house." He is here to remind you of the mission you forgot. You are weeping now, ashamed. He is not interested in your tears. Now that you remember your contract, you are required to fulfill it.

This is my own version of a story I feel I am living. You'll find versions in sources ranging from the Gnostic Hymn of the Pearl to Doris Lessing's novel *Shikasta*. Perhaps it will speak to you too. I find it useful to believe (as Plato believed) that each of us agreed to a contract before we came into this world in our present bodies. The trick is to remember the terms of that sacred contract and then to find the courage and constancy to fulfill them. I am grateful for the night, long ago, when I heard a knock on my door in the middle of the night and opened it to find a young man outside, his face shining like the moon. He said, "I come from my father's house." And the dream was more real than the life I had been living in this sublunary world.

You Must Tell Your Story and Have It Received

"The world can't end," writes Michael Meade, "unless it runs out of stories. For this world is made of stories, each tale a part of an eternal drama being told from beginning to end over and over again. As long as all the stories don't come to an end the world will continue."[20]

Scheherazade tells stories so she may live through another night, and tells them so well she turns a monstrous tyrant into a decent human being. The Irish storyteller beautifully evoked by Ruth Sawyer in *The Way of the Storyteller* tells stories so "each may find something for which his soul had cried out" or "to keep the heart warm in a country a long distance from an Irish turf fire."[21]

You must know your story and tell your story and have your story received. This is a central teaching of the Sefer Yetzirah, a seminal text of Kabbalah. Learn to do that, and you can survive the worst nightmares of history and bring heart and healing to others, as we'll learn in the next chapter.

12

Dreamgrowing in Auschwitz

Every human being has the freedom to change at any instant.
— VIKTOR FRANKL, *Man's Search for Meaning*

He has been reduced to a number tattooed on his arm. His ability to survive until tomorrow depends on being able to dig stones for a long day without collapsing from malnutrition and fatigue, and on being able to get a few peas at the bottom of a bowl of soup, and on not falling foul of one of the SS guards or the no less brutal Capos, fellow prisoners selected to act as wardens and help choose who will be sent to the "bathhouse" that leads to the crematorium. He reaches into the storehouse of memory for images that can help him to live. He cherishes little things from the life that has been taken from him, like taking a bus ride, or turning on the lights in his apartment, or finding real food in the kitchen. Most of all, he cherishes the image of his wife. He doesn't know whether she is still alive, but the great love between them is real and helps to sustain him.

When he can get scraps of paper, he tries to reconstruct the book manuscript that was torn from him by a Capo when he came here. He dreams of seeing it published. In the indeterminate state of a death camp prisoner, with no way of knowing whether he will live or die within the next hour, he *chooses* to grow a vision of the future in his mind. It is an extraordinary vision, and it takes a terrific act of will for him to turn his mind from his bleeding feet and aching stomach and inhabit a future that very few could begin to imagine. The emaciated prisoner of Auschwitz transports himself to a warm and comfortable lecture room, in a civilized time and place in which the horrors of World War II lie in the past. The speaker is the prisoner himself, Dr. Viktor Frankl. From the platform, he surveys an attentive audience seated on handsomely upholstered chairs. His topic? *The psychology of the concentration camp.*

After his release from Auschwitz and the fall of the Third Reich, Frankl recalled the effect of this remarkable exercise in active imagination. "All that oppressed me in that moment became objective, seen and described from the remote viewpoint of science. By this method I succeeded somehow in rising above the situation, above the sufferings of the moment, and I observed them as if they were already of the past. Both I and my troubles became the object of an interesting psychoscientific study undertaken by myself."[22]

This is a stellar example of the power of dreamgrowing — of developing a creative vision powerful enough to carry you beyond adversity. Inside one of the worst of history's nightmares, Frankl reclaimed the identity and the future that had been torn from him. He not only saw himself surviving the death camps; he also saw himself emerging to found a new approach to psychology on what he had learned from them. In doing this, he stepped outside and above his appalling circumstances to adopt the perspective of a witness and a scientist. He transported himself to a future time in which the hideous collective nightmare was in the past. In doing this, he succeeded in escaping, mentally, from the camp. But he did more: he reached so powerfully for a possible future that it seems an answering force helped to pull him toward it.

Whatever the pain and adversity of our lives, we can all take heart from Viktor Frankl's tremendous example. Even when all other freedoms are denied us — he later insisted — we can never lose the final freedom, the freedom to choose our *attitude.* We can choose to give up or to struggle on. We can choose to find meaning in our suffering or to pronounce our world unfair and meaningless (as too many people do under circumstances that look quite comfortable to most of the world's poor, let alone a death camp inmate). It is our choice. If we choose to believe that we have no choice, we are still making a choice. If Frankl could say yes to life in Auschwitz and, even there, find meaning in what life threw at him, who are we to go about with the misery-guts attitude that life is unfair or meaningless?

Frankl founded the method he called logotherapy, sometimes described as the third of the great Viennese schools of psychology (after Freud's and Adler's). As the name suggests, this is therapy based on the need for *logos*, or meaning. The central thesis is that many of our ailments are *noögenic* — that is to say, they have their origin in the realm of *noös*, or mind, rather than in the psyche as observed by psychiatrists, or the body as diagnosed by physicians. The human animal needs *meaning* as well as food and air and sex and water. The sense that life is meaningless is at the root of a great deal of depression, aggression, and addiction, which can only be addressed by a restoration of the sense that life is meaning-full.

How do we find meaning in our lives? We find it in work, especially in creative action. We find it as we engage in the world and with other people. We find it — Frankl insisted over and over — in the attitude we adopt in the face of unavoidable suffering. Let me add that we also find meaning in our engagement with our dreams. Our dreams, and the powers that speak to us in dreams, are forever inviting us to reclaim the knowledge of who we are, why we are here, and what our purpose is in our current life experience.

I read *Man's Search for Meaning* when I was a student. I've read it three times since, and I expect I'll read it again. It offers perennial wisdom. Frankl deploys several of my favorite quotes, which are relevant to his theme.

From Nietzsche, he borrows this celebrated and telling truth: "He who has a *why* to live can cope with almost any *how*."

From Dostoyevsky, this: "My only fear in life is of not being worthy of my suffering."

From Spinoza: "Suffering ceases to be suffering as soon as we produce a clear and precise picture of it."

And then he quotes the Viennese writer Arthur Schnitzler, a contemporary of Freud. Schnitzler maintained that there are really only three virtues, which he itemized as follows: objectivity, courage, and the sense of responsibility. An interesting choice.

We saw something of the merit of "objectivity" in the way Frankl was able to take himself out of his situation in the death camp and look down — and back — from the viewpoint of a scientific observer. Courage, certainly, is a fundamental virtue. It is not the absence of fear; that could be psychosis or reckless stupidity. Courage is fear conquered by something stronger than fear, by love, or belief, or duty, or a cause. The sense of responsibility — of being responsible for our own lives, first and last, and for exercising our power to choose our responses to whatever life gives us — is clearly of vital importance in a life that meets the existential challenge, said Frankl: "Ultimately, man should not ask what the meaning of his life is, but rather he must recognize that it is he who is asked. In a word, each man is questioned by life; and he can only answer to life by answering for his own life; to life he can only respond by being responsible."[23]

Not a bad exercise, in our own quest for meaning, to name the three virtues that count the most in our own experience. Whatever selection we make, for me — as for Frankl (in the death camp, thinking of his beloved wife) — the fundament of all is *love*. This is what makes us human and sustains us daily, even when we dare not say its name.

Dreamgrowing means developing a creative vision that wants to take root in our world and is strong enough to carry us beyond adversity. Whatever our circumstances, we can all take heart from Viktor Frankl's tremendous example. Even when all other freedoms are denied us, we can never lose the final freedom, the freedom to choose our *attitude*. We can choose to give up or to struggle on. We can choose to find meaning in our suffering, or to pronounce our world unfair and meaningless.

Dreamgrowing for Each Other

We can help to grow a dream — a healing image, a life vision, perhaps a pathway to the next world — for someone in need of a dream. Dream

Transfer is a powerful and innovative technique that has emerged from my teaching and practice over many years.

The prerequisite for Dream Transfer is to establish a safe and supportive personal space where we can talk to someone in need of help and guidance. We define the core theme for which that person would like support, get some background on his life circumstances, and seek a gateway image that will help us to enter his personal space. We then proceed to *grow a vision for him.*

The dream we grow may be one of our own life memories, the returning memory of a personal dream, an intuitive flash, or a series of images born fresh in our space. If the dream involves challenging or disturbing content, we always go through this and beyond it, opening paths to resolution and healing. We allow the dream to develop into a vivid scene and explore it with all our inner senses. Then we share the dream we have found and invite the other person to step inside it and explore its scenery. The dream beneficiary now tells the dream as his own dream and claims its landscapes and its energy.

This process has proven to be deeply healing and rewarding in many situations. It is easily learned, and quickly brings our natural intuitive abilities richly alive. Dream Transfer is especially powerful in helping the dying to move beyond fear and to approach the last stages of life as an opportunity for personal growth and direct connection with sources of wisdom in a deeper reality. It is a method for helping those in our world who do not have a dream — a life dream or a dream of the night — to open their personal doorways to insight, healing, and a deeper life.

Let me share a personal account of dreamgrowing for a man with a life-threatening illness. I'll recount this exactly as it unfolded in the midst of an active dreamer's life.

Time for the Shark God

He is on a field of battle, facing a host of freakish ogres like the orcs in *Lord of the Rings.* His strength is failing. He can never slay all of these monsters.

He wakes in terror, his body wracked with pain. He takes more of the pills the doctors have given him. They make him groggy and foggy without taking away the pain.

He forces his stooped and twisted body out onto the deck and collapses into a lounger. Out here, on the edge of summer in Calistoga, California, the hot, dry Santa Ana winds carry the smell of burning, the smell of ash. Like the ash that is killing him. After thirty years of cigarette smoking, he has developed lung cancer. When they found the cancer — after misdiagnosing it as pneumonia — the doctors told him the cancer had metastasized. It was in his bones, in his liver, in his marrow.

"How much time?" he asked them. They did not want to say. "How much time?" he insisted. "I have to know." They told him: "One or two months."

When he closes his eyes out there in the burning wind, he sees the monstrous legions again. Mindless and unstoppable, their sole purpose to eat him alive.

In the midst of a coughing fit that makes his lungs ache and bends him double, he calls for help. He has the impression, in the horrific scene that is still playing out in his mind, that he has an ally. A friend has entered the field. He cannot make out the shape or features of his ally, but the sense is strong enough to give him a breath of hope, a patch of fresh air on the smoking lip of the volcano.

His name was Peter. He had been a professional actor on Broadway and had nearly made it onto the marquees, until his wife left him and he could not stand to live in New York anymore without her. He had earned good money, met glamorous people, and lived the good life as a master sommelier in California's wine country. He had always worked out and taken good care of his body, except for the cigarettes. And he was just fifty-four.

I had never heard his name until I received a call for help near midnight on Friday, May 11, 2007, one week after Peter's dream of the evil hosts on the field of battle.

The man who called was Peter's cousin, a friend who knew I had done some imaginal healing with cancer patients. He wondered if I could do anything for Peter. Peter was on the other side of the country, in Calistoga. But maybe I could call him and talk to him on the phone.

I tend to avoid the phone and rarely do work with people who are previously unknown to me. But twin synchronicities came into play now, and I allowed them to guide me. I had just sent a friend an email mentioning Calistoga — a place I had never visited — because of a dream about a petrified forest (there's a famous one just outside Calistoga). Next, and irresistible for me, when the phone rang I was reading a book called *The Shark God*. The book is a Pacific travelogue; the title refers to an encounter with an island saltwater shaman who works with the shark spirit.

What's the connection here? The shark does not get cancer.

The *idea* of the shark can help people who are challenged by the disease. I have found many times over the years that the shark can be a powerful imaginal ally in these waters. If you can picture the shark swimming through your body devouring the cells of your disease, you can do yourself some real good. The more strongly you can see and feel and believe that the shark is with you and inside you, the more good you can do.

You can start by pretending. Do that well enough and you may move beyond make-believe to the belief that can change everything. Call the shark inside you, and you may find that what has come is more than a picture. The greatest challenges call the greatest allies. If your need and your courage are great enough, you may even find you have called a shark god.

"Let me dream on this," I told the midnight caller.

The Hawaiians say the night is the time of the gods. I would let the night reveal what was possible for Peter.

The warrior giant is dripping, as if he has just stepped out of the ocean. He is magnificent, naked except for the tattoos on his cheeks. He rears in front of me, snorting and grunting. His eyes roll back, and for a moment I can see only the whites in place of the shiny, jet-black pupils. He goes down on his haunches, grunting and panting, and sticks his tongue out until the pointy tip curls under his chin.

He produces something that looks like an ax, except it is carved from hardwood. The end flares out, making the shape of a triangular axhead. Beneath it, points protrude like shark's teeth.

The giant brandishes his war club in a series of rapid and complex motions, slicing and chopping, hacking and sweeping. He wants me to see something beyond the motions. What is it? He is cutting dark things out of my energy field. Shadowy, stringy things. Dead energies, rotting cords of attachment.

He bellows and hurls his club at me. I manage to catch it by the shaft. Its weight and velocity have me staggering back a few steps.

I grasp the giant's intention. He wants me to reproduce his movements. This takes several trials. When he seems satisfied, I move to return the war club. This is not what he wants. What am I to do with this club fanged with shark's teeth?

I know now. I am to store it inside my solar plexus. The power will live in my body now and will be available to others.

Who are you? I want to know.

I am the brother of fire. I am Pele's older brother.

This was the return of an old vision, which was weaving itself on the loom of night into newer visions. I had danced into the original vision nine years earlier while fumbling hula steps in a circle of dancers under a thatched roof on the wild northern coast of Oahu in 1998.

The original vision was kinesthetic as much as visual. It infused me with a sense of surging power that was firmly seated in my body. I did not know — at first — that I had met Pele's brother.

I talked about my vision later that day with friends from the mainland while strolling through the lobby of the Turtle Bay Hilton. I noticed some war clubs for sale in the gift shop and went in to see if any of the clubs resembled the one from my vision. I was impressed by the quality of the objects on display. Though presumably made for the tourist trade and scaled down in size, they looked like authentic, even museum-quality replicas. But there was nothing on the wall resembling my vision club.

I stopped at the counter and asked a friendly Polynesian woman about what I had seen. She asked me to draw the club from my vision. When she looked at the sketch, she grinned broadly, reached down below the counter, and produced a hardwood war club that was an exact copy of the one in my vision, except that it was scaled down to half size.

"My nephew carved this," the woman told me. "He brought it in just to-day. This one is used to cut a pathway between the worlds."

When I purchased the club, she cautioned me, "Now a spirit of Ha-waii will always be inside you, and you will come back to us."

I went back a year later. Lying on white sand on a deserted beach soon after sunrise, I watched a silver shark nose in close to the shore. At the moment it seemed about to slide out of the water, it became a grace-ful, silvery woman. She lay with me there on the white sand. She was lovely, but her eyes were those of the shark. The encounter was so vivid in the morning light that I scanned the beach and the nearby houses to see if anyone was watching us. I knew — without words, as just-so knowing — that after this the shark would always be close to me.

During that same trip, I drove the zigzag road — ten thousand feet straight up from sea level — to the crater of the dormant volcano on Maui. I found I needed to walk that landscape with great reverence; I was moving on the sleeping body of a goddess. Noticing my care, a young Hawaiian woman, a park ranger, struck up a conversation. She told me I must not leave the island without a copy of Martha Beckwith's *Hawaiian Mythology*. "She was a Victorian gentlewoman, pure Seven Sisters — went to school at Mount Holyoke, taught at Smith — but she tended and translated the stories of my people like no other. Our kahu-nas read her." I found a copy of the book, first published in 1940, and saw it was full of stories of the shark god in his many forms.

On my return to the mainland, I was called on to help a number of people who were challenged by cancer. Again and again, I found myself encouraging them to visualize a shark swimming through their bodies, devouring the cells of their disease and excreting the sickness cleanly. In many cases, the people who were able to receive the shark fully — as a vivid image in their mind and their inner senses — were able to mobi-lize tremendous powers for self-healing.

Then a woman friend who often assisted me in healing work had a dream of her own. She saw a magnificent Polynesian warrior figure brandishing a war club studded with shark's teeth. He told her he was Pele's brother.

She was vaguely aware that Pele was a fierce fire goddess of Hawaii, associated with a volcano, but knew nothing about a brother of Pele. I got out the Beckwith book and quickly confirmed that not only does Pele have a brother, but he is also one of the most important avatars of the shark god. His name is Kamohoali'i. Many places in the islands are sacred to him, including a cliff just above the crater of Kilauea, the fiery, smoking volcano on the Big Island. Thanks to his sister, the smoke of the volcano never touches his sanctuary on the high cliff.

He owns a secret land deep beneath the ocean where the regenerative power of the Water of Life can be sought by those who have the courage and stamina to go deep enough.[24]

The morning after the midnight call, I took down the war club I had brought back from Oahu. It usually hangs on a wall near the desk where I write.

Without thinking, I found myself reproducing the motions the warrior giant had shown me, cutting and stripping, combing and sweeping. I added new movements, rasping the carved shark's teeth across the nape of my neck, beating the flat of the triangular head across my shoulder blades.

A story was growing in me, deeper and stronger, with these body movements. Who knew what this story might accomplish if it could live in another man's body, adapted to his life, his tastes, and his needs?

I knew what to do.

I phoned Peter.

We established some common ground. He knew the power of story. He agreed that the body believes in images. He had been an actor on Broadway and had embodied some big dramas. He did not wish to die the way he had been told he would die. "I want to live, and I am ready to fight."

No, I did not need to hear his medical history or his prognosis.

I wanted to hear his dreams.

He said, "In my dreams, I am facing a host of monsters, like the things in *Lord of the Rings*."

"Are you ready to accept an ally?"

"I would love that."

"Then I have a story for you. Would you like to hear it?"

"More than anything."

I held the war club as I spoke. I started by taking him back to the place of terror he had dreamed.

"You are facing a host of monstrous beings. You are exhausted by the fight against terrible odds. Your enemies are unstoppable, and their only desire is to consume you.

"But now you realize you are not alone. Your ally has stepped into the field. Do you see him?"

"Oh, yes. Thank God."

"He is a giant, and he is magnificent. He is built like a immense Polynesian warrior. Water streams from his skin as if he has just stepped out of the ocean. He is brandishing a great war club. You notice the club is studded with shark's teeth. Do you see it?"

"Yes. I'm there."

"He is routing and *devouring* your adversaries. As he slashes through their ranks, swinging his club, you have the impression of tremendous snapping jaws. He is an impeccable killing machine. Your enemies have no chance against him."

"I can see it. I'm there."

"But now your ally — let's call him the Shark Guy — is coming at you. He's mad as hell, he's pissed. He's snarling and coming at you with that damn club. He's hacking and slicing. You hear the hiss as he beats the air around you. You feel the shark's teeth rasping and ripping at your skin. You realize that, with his blows, he is sweeping away dark strands in your energy field that you had not noticed until now. These dark energy cords have connected you to dead things from your past — to old attachments that have been draining and confusing your energies. To old grief and guilt and shame. And to *dead smokers* who have inflicted their symptoms as well as their addictions on you."

"Oh, God." Peter was sobbing now. "This is big. This is tremendous."

"Do you feel those dead connections — those dead smokers — being cut away?"

"Yes, yes! I feel it. It's happening!"

"You are being released from all of that. Are you letting it go?"

He was crying his heart out. "Yes."

He started thanking me, over and over.

"Peter, the Shark Guy isn't done with you. He wants you to take the war club. Can you do that?"

"I'm taking it."

"He wants you to make the same motions he did. He wants you to chop and hack and saw and sweep, and feel *yourself* getting all the crud off, and out."

"Wait. I'm going outside."

I waited as he dragged his body outside with the phone. Through a new bout of coughing, he gasped, "I'm outside in the same hot winds that were blowing when those — *things* — were trying to destroy me. I'm chopping — HAH! — and scraping — AARRGH! — and I'm sweeping the crap away. And I'm breathing. Oh, God, I'm breathing."

He was taking the story into his body. I listened to him gasping and panting and grunting for a long time. When we were both satisfied he had done all that was required, I said firmly, "Peter, there's more. The Shark Guy wants you to take that club into your body. Can you feel yourself taking it into your gut, into your solar plexus?"

"It's already there."

"Now something amazing is happening. That club is becoming a shark. The shark is swimming through all of your body — through your cell system — and he is snapping and chomping, eating up the cells of your disease. Are you feeling that?"

"Yes. It hurts like hell, but it also feels wonderful."

"Okay. So let the shark go wherever he needs to go — and let him do this again and again later on."

I could have ended the story here, at least for now, but the knowledge that this Shark Guy was the brother of fire had gripped me with a fierce sense of further possibilities. I was going to dare Peter to seize them.

"Peter?"

"I'm here. And the shark is inside me."

"You are going to allow the shark into your lungs."

Peter howled. It was hard to separate all the emotions — pain and fear and relief and wild hope — that might be riding on that scream.

"Is the shark there?

"Yes."

"Peter, this Shark Guy is the brother of fire. We can talk later about what this means. For now, let him take you on a journey, starting from the place where you have been burned, to another place of fire. You are swimming with the shark — *like* the shark — across the ocean."

"I'm there."

"It feels fabulous to be streaming with the ocean. You feel the power of your muscles as you surge through the water. You are swimming with delight toward a far island. There is a volcano on the island. You rise up, and now you are above the crater of the volcano. You are on a high cliff. You look down into the crater, which is smoking and steaming and bubbling with lava, and you see...a colossal ashtray."

Peter sounded like he was dry-retching. Choking, he said, "I'm there."

"But where you are now, all that smoke and ash can no longer touch you. You stand strong on a high place, and the clean winds are blowing across your skin and streaming through your lungs. You can breathe. You are in a place where smoke and ash cannot touch you, because you are the brother of fire. Can you claim this place?"

For the first time, a hesitancy. "I'm trying."

"You will come here again. And we can see it from a different angle. For now, I want you to make one last journey. Are you game for that?"

"Absolutely."

"The Shark Guy is the owner of a hidden island. It is hidden deep beneath the ocean, at the sunrise end of the world. If you can get down there, you can drink the Water of Life and claim the power of regeneration. Are you willing to try?"

"Take me there. Please."

"You are swimming again, like a shark, toward the rising light. Now you are plunging and diving down deep, deeper that you ever thought it was possible to go. Can you do that?"

"I'm trying. Give me a moment. I'm almost there."

"You are plunging deeper and deeper, and you have no trouble breathing. It's amazing, and beautiful."

"I'm there."

"You are going to drink the Water of Life, Peter. Its taste on your palate is finer than the finest wine you have ever drunk. Do you taste it yet?"

He moaned with pleasure.

"You feel the Water of Life — with all its potency for regeneration and rejuvenation — streaming through every fiber of your being. Do you accept its power?"

"With every part of me."

Time to bring him back. I was awed by how far and how deep he had gone.

"You are gently returning to the surface — to your self — shining and strong, deliciously intoxicated, filled with delight. Everything will be different now."

His breath, over the line, sounded like a prayer.

"So, Peter, that is the story I wanted to give you. I invite you to take any part of it you want and make it fully your own."

"I take all of it."

"Then tell it back to yourself in your own way. You may want to record your own version in your own voice. You'll want to go back inside each scene. You are a brilliant performer, and you'll want to enter the role you have been given and make this the greatest performance of your life."

"I will do all of that. I will claim the power of the Shark Guy. Whatever happens in my life and death, I will be stronger and better. This is the greatest gift I have ever received."

Less than six weeks later, on June 22, I received extraordinary news. Peter's cousin called to report that Peter had just been declared almost completely cancer-free. The disease was virtually gone from his liver, his bone cancer had vanished, and the spots on his lungs had shrunk until they were almost undetectable. "This is miracle-grade news," I was told. "It looks like he's going to be a survivor."

His remission may have been the effect of chemotherapy and ex-perimental drugs, as Peter's doctors maintained. For his part, Peter told us he believed that one of the great factors in his healing was that he had been gripped by the sense of a "big story" and a "big purpose."

The big story helped to save him from cancer. Then he was called elsewhere. His immune system had been badly damaged by the disease and the chemicals, and a month after his doctors told him he had beaten the cancer, he succumbed to pneumonia.

I reopened *The Shark God*, the book that, through fine synchronic-ity, had keyed me into what needed to be done the night Peter's cousin reached to me for help. It is wonderfully well written by an adventur-ous Canadian called Charles Montgomery, whose great-grandfather had been a missionary in Melanesia.

The author has this to say about mythical thinking: "When you fall toward mythical thinking, when you rub up against the rough edges of it long enough, it can enter you like a virus, and the world changes. There is more danger, but there is more possibility. Events present themselves symbolically. They wrap themselves in magic…and their circumstances assume direction and purpose."[25]

When we are seized by the big story, we step beyond limiting defini-tions and beliefs. Great healing becomes possible because we can now draw on the immense energy that becomes available when we know we are serving a larger purpose.

True shamans have always known this, and one of their most effec-tive modes of healing is to weave a story with mythic power around a sufferer, a story that can inhabit his body and mind and give him the courage and stamina to get through.

The death of the body is no defeat if we have found our bigger story. The terrible failure is to live and die bereft of the sense of a greater drama that fires us up to give more than we thought possible.

Peter rose beyond fear and pain when he let himself be seized by a bigger story. I like to think its power travels with him on the immense journey on which he is now embarked. *There is more danger, but more possibility.*

EXERCISE FOR PARTNERS

Dream Transfer

- Open a safe space.
- Set the intention and open a gateway.
- As the intended beneficiary, you need to give the dreamgrower just three things:

  - *An intention.* Briefly describe a major issue on which you would like help or guidance.

  - *Just enough personal background* for the dreamgrower to understand the context, and the resources and challenges available to you.

  - *A gateway image.* This may be a dream, a life memory, or a symptom. What comes to mind when you focus on your issue? The picture you produce will give the dreamgrower a gateway through which to enter your space.

- Guidance for the dreamgrower on your assignment:

  - Via active imagination, you are going to grow a vision for your partner that will offer positive guidance or healing. Don't hesitate to draw on your personal dreams and life memories while growing the dream you will bring back. If you run into challenging material, it is your task to find a path to a happy outcome.

- Guidance for the dreamgrower on the transfer:

  - After the journey, you will sit with your partner and ask her permission to tell her the dream you have brought. You want to tell it with sensual, sensory detail so she can taste it, touch it, smell it, and wrap it around herself. At the end of the telling, you will invite the beneficiary to take any part of the dream she wants and to make it her own by telling it back to you, with herself at the center of the action.

- Guidance for the beneficiary:

  - Your job is to stay focused on your intention and on creating a warm and welcoming space in yourself for the gift that will be brought to you. You may want to sit or lie so you are touching your partner lightly. Let the dreamgrower do the work.

- Drumming for the journey (optional but recommended). If one of you is able and willing to drum, use live drumming. Otherwise, use a drumming CD (see the "Resources" section).
- After the recall, the dreamgrower initiates the Dream Transfer by telling a story.
- The beneficiary makes the dream her own by recounting part or all of the dream in her own way, making any changes she likes, claiming the energy for herself.
- Action plan: partners agree on an action plan to honor the dream that now belongs to the beneficiary of the Dream Transfer.

Some questions about this process that are likely to arise:

Q. Am I making this up?

A. Maybe so — and it's fine to make it up if the effect is to bring through positive energy and healing. In modern society, we underrate the creative power of imagination — the great faculty of soul — just as we underrate dreams.

Q. Is it possible that I got all sorts of psychic "hits," which my partner confirmed?

A: Sure. The fact that you have just "seen" your partner's childhood home, or "heard" the name of his uncle in Boston, helps confirm that you are on the right page. But don't get overexcited; your psychic faculties are running strong because you have been invited into someone's space (and anyway, we are all "psychic" and all connected). You are doing something vastly more important and interesting than a psychic reading: you are bringing energy and imagery to empower and heal.

Q: Is this projection?

A: Absolutely! But it is radically different from the swamp of unconscious and often negative projections that confuse so many of us in ordinary life. This is intentional, hyperconscious positive projection, performed with full and informed consent.

13

Tracking the Synchron-O-city Beast

Nothing happens in which you are not entangled in a secret manner, for everything has ordered itself around you and plays your innermost. Nothing in you is hidden to things.... The stars whisper your deepest mysteries to you, and the soft valleys of the earth rescue you in a motherly womb.

— CARL JUNG, *The Red Book*

Shhhh. If you're quiet for a moment, you'll hear him snuffling and padding around the room. Most grown-ups can't hear him or see him, because they are too busy. Whatever age you are, you don't want to miss him. When *he's* around, things happen differently. You can finish something before you started it, which is really cool when it comes to doing chores.

He is, of course, the Synchron-O-city Beast. I shall tell you exactly how he got his name and his shape. There was once a very clever professor in Switzerland who woke up noticing what you and I know but most grown-ups forget: coincidence *matters*, terribly. But it was very hard for him to explain this to respectable adults in a country of bankers and cuckoo clocks, so he made up a word that sounded scientific. The word was *synchronicity*, which he defined as "an acausal connecting principle." He was talking about meaningful coincidence. You and I know that coincidence *always* means something. It's through coincidence that we discover that the world inside us and the world outside us aren't really separate. It's through coincidence that we discover the secret doors to the world-behind-the-world that open in our dreams but often seem to be bricked over in the daytime, as if they were never there. Through co-incidence, we discover that there are players involved in our games of life who live on the other side of the curtain between the worlds, but who can reach through that curtain to move a piece on the board, or tickle us, or muss our hair.

The Swiss professor got serious people — the sort who would never listen to talk of "coincidence" — to sit through his lectures when he sub-stituted the word *synchronicity*. He also got them to listen because he told good stories about how synchronicity worked in his own life, about how a solid cabinet cracked with a loud BANG when he was getting into an argument with his own teacher, or how a fox appeared on a path when he was talking to a lady about a dream of a fox.

I have never liked the word *synchronicity* as much as that good old word *coincidence*. But alas, *coincidence* has been horribly "ad-justed" and "only-fied" by all the people who have long been in the habit of saying "just coincidence" or "only coincidence." It has even been "not-ified" by people who insist it's "not coincidence" when they really mean that it is, when it's something real and important and meaningful and they don't understand (because of the bad talk they've learned) that coincidence is all of those things.

So I've been using the word *synchronicity* in my writings and classes. But in one of those classes was a sweet lady artist who could never say it quite right. It always came out "synchron-O-city" with a great big O where an *i* should be. I thought this was rather cute and couldn't bear to correct her. So, month after month, following her homeplay assignments, she would bring us tales of synchron-O-city, to our smiling delight.

One evening there was a newcomer in the class, a serious person and a stickler for accuracy in everything that can be looked up.

"I have another synchron-O-city to tell," said the lady artist, eager to share.

"You mean synchron-*i*-city," said the newcomer. "You should get it right."

Crestfallen, the artist tried to correct herself but faltered.

I quickly intervened. "*Please* don't ever change the way you say that word," I implored the artist. "Every time you say it, I sense a soft, snuffly animal — the Synchron-O-city Beast — coming into the room."

I paused. In that moment, I believe we all heard and sensed something like a plush baby rhino snuffling and snorting. The First Peoples of the country where I grew up, Down Under, say that to name something is to bring it into the world. The Synchron-O-city Beast is now alive and ever so busy in this world.

I can prove this because, soon after this incident, a writer called Maureen reported a most delightful dream in which she is one of a team of counselors helping me to run a camp for children where we supervise sleepover parties and dream together. Padding and snuffling all over the magical house in the woods where we are gathered is a creature she describes as a "baby rhino," soft and cuddly. I don't think Maureen ever heard of the Synchron-O-city Beast from me, at least not in an ordinary way. The Synchron-O-city Beast just went ahead and introduced himself. I hope they are feeding him well in Maureen's dream camp. He thrives on giggles and slips of the tongue. He likes to exercise by shredding the curtain of solemn people's expectations and butting holes into Outland and Fairyland and other lands big enough to be doorways for anyone with a child's sense of wonder. And he always shows up when we play the Coincidence Card Game.

The Index Card Oracle

This is one of my favorite games, suitable not only for workshops but also for any social gathering where people are ready to think outside the box. I get everyone in the circle to write something — a summary of a dream, an incident from memory, a reflection, or a favorite quote — on one side of a three-by-five index card, as legibly as possible. We gather the cards into a deck. I then ask everyone to write down an intention for guidance, expressing this as simply and clearly as possible ("I would like guidance on…"). I then go around the circle, offering the deck. Everyone pulls a card at random.

The game requires us to pretend that whatever is written on the card is a direct message from the universe in response to the intention for guidance. The message may be obscure or ambiguous but, hey, that's how oracles stay in business long-term.

As a divination deck, our Coincidence Cards can't be beat. We come up with a one-time deck, exclusively for us, that will never be used in this form again. Of course, some of the messages are "keepers." My journals are stuffed with index cards whose inscriptions remind me of big dreams and coincidence fugues, of wildly funny incidents, and of moments of insight and epiphany when we punched a hole in the surface world and saw into a deeper order of reality.

I've been looking over my collection of Coincidence Cards, and I'll share some of the messages here without attempting to recall the specific meanings that each of them assumed in the context of the intentions. Notes from the dreamworld include:

> I'm in a wedding procession. As we walk down the aisle and step up to the altar, I realize we have entered a diner.

> Circus elephants circle around linked trunk to tail, lovingly, caringly giving each other a way to follow. Each is a leader as much as a follower.

> I'm in a large room where we each have to fly up to the ceiling every two or three minutes to breathe, as if the room is underwater.

> The moon goddess stands in her majesty above the Sea of Tranquility. She is flanked by her armored moon soldiers and carried on the back of a giant crab moving gently through the sea.

> The dragon sits on your shoulder. His fire breath drives back the dark.

Two men are taking me to my execution by beheading. I fight until my mother appears and tells me it will be okay. I submit myself to the execution and I am happy.

A jaguar leaps out of the forest and into the driver's seat of a pink Firebird convertible. It morphs into a cartoon version of itself, puts on sunglasses, and drives away, waving as it says, "Hasta la vista."

Some of the messages come from observations on the roads of everyday life:

My daughter hands me the feather of a blue heron and tells me I will need it this weekend.

A red passion flower lying in the roadway all alone.

A death's-head skull is floating in midair. I look for its origin and find that it is the reflection of a pattern on a woman's purse.

A salmon pink trumpetlike flower opens before my eyes, bursting with joyful life!

Some of the cards contain insights harvested from the workshops:

You do not need to hunt your power. Your power will hunt you. Find a sacred space where your power can find you.

Throw out your net and fish in the River of Dreams.

The child does not need to grow up to be complete.

In playing the Coincidence Card Game, we sometimes draw our own card, which is statistically improbable and often very interesting. It suggests, for one thing, that you already have the answer. You don't need to look outside yourself, only to go deeper within.

More Coincidence Games

"Even the stones speak to you," Jung wrote in his *Red Book,* "and magical threads spin from you to things and from things to you."[26] In the speaking land, everything will speak to us if we are willing to listen.

Letting the World Put Its Question to You

My favorite way of navigating by synchronicity is simply to accept the first unusual or striking thing that enters my perception on any given day as a signal from the world, a possible clue to what *wants* to happen

An excellent game to play, as an active dreamer in everyday life, is to schedule ten minutes (or more) of *unscheduled* time, at the place of your choosing, and, using all of your senses, spend that time scanning whatever is going on in the world around you.

By doing so, we receive a benefit similar to the gift of spontaneous night dreams, one that brings into consciousness many things we have not previously considered. And we can experience a quality of *objectivity* that is often lacking when we are trying to control or program inner experience. Similarly, the questions the world puts to us via the spontaneous play of synchronicity can be even more interesting than the results we get when we put our questions to the world.

Personal Omens

I'm in favor of *practical* superstitions, by which I mean developing a set of personal omens that actually deliver. I decided long ago that, for me, a friendly black dog — especially when sighted under unusual circumstances — is a good omen. So too, for me, is the appearance of a red-tailed hawk, especially when flying my way. Both have given me reliable signs on memorable occasions. But if I find that things go amiss after future sightings, I'll revise my personal superstitions. As Jung said, "The real is what works."

Sounds out of Silence

The ancient Greeks regarded a *kledon* — a sound out of silence, or the first words heard at a new location — as one of the most valuable oracles.

I had a personal experience of a *kledon* while working on this book. I was changing planes at Chicago's Midway airport. I arrived at the Southwest Airlines gate to find there was nowhere to sit while waiting, so I took my place in the spot where the line would begin forming. (Southwest doesn't issue seat assignments but numbers in the wait-line to get on board.) Because I was standing there early, I heard a woman lecturing a group of moms and high school seniors with some passion: "Listen up! You need to know this. I was reading about how success isn't a result of being smart. You need some smarts, but success really depends on being able to make a statement, to tell your story."

Now this is — exactly — a major theme in this book, and what I was planning to discuss at dinner with my editor the following evening. So I was excited that this was my *kledon* at that airport. When the woman returned from a restroom stop, she flashed me a smile and I seized the chance to say, "I heard you saying that in order to succeed in life, we need to learn to tell our story so other people can hear it and receive it. That is absolutely right." In high excitement, she said, "Will you say that to these guys? Maybe they'll get it, coming from you." So I said it again, improvising and adding a little, developing text that is now in this book.

Shelf Elves

Arthur Koestler spoke of the Library Angel — that bookish spirit that makes texts appear at just the right time. I wish to speak now of a lesser, but highly active, spirit of the stacks that we may call the shelf elf. He not only makes books turn up in unexpected ways but can also hide them or even make them disappear.

He is often at play in my preferred bookshops, which tend to be quirky independents and havens of twice-sold tales. One of these shelf elf–haunted establishments is just down the street from my home, which is a mixed blessing because, in the course of a year, a significant portion of this bookshop's stock migrates up the street to my house.

It was in this bookshop that I found the meaning of a funny dream word (*chantepleure*) in a book placed at eye level from my point of vision at the door, so I could not fail to see it and was, thereby, drawn into transtemporal intrigues involving a poet-prince of Orléans in whose name Joan of Arc went to war.

It was there, over the holidays, that I repaired with the feeling that there was something by Jorge Luis Borges that I urgently needed to read that day. Newly arrived, casually dropped on top of a short stack in the literature section, was an English translation of *The Book of Sand*, which I naturally purchased. I opened this collection of Borges's later stories and was immediately engrossed in a tale ("The Other") in which Borges meets a much younger self on a bench. Borges tells his younger self what life will bring him over the forty years that divide them. The young Borges, who believes he is dreaming, will forget the information he has received from his older self, letting it fade like a dream. This tale weaves together two of my favorite themes, the many varieties of the double and the relativity of time, and I was grateful to the shelf elf who put it in front of me.

Of Gatekeepers

I arrived at my local airport at 5:30 AM on a Sunday, checked my bag, and got in line for the security check. Before I handed her my driver's license and boarding pass, the female TSA agent who was doing the document scan greeted me by name, like an old friend: "Well, hello, Robert!" Her Southern accent was familiar and so was her warm, smiling face. I recognized a woman who had been a member of one of my monthly evening circles more than a decade before. She had entertained us with wonderful stories of growing up in the rural South and of dream travels to ghost villages and other locations that are not on airline itineraries. "How come you're working here?" I asked her. She replied, "I was dreaming about airports so much I decided I might as well work at one."

It felt like a very good start to the day, to meet a gatekeeper who is also a dreamer. The Gatekeeper is a very important figure in my imaginal life. In dreams, the Gatekeeper may appear as a generic figure familiar on the roads of regular life — the customs officer, the ticket collector, the security guard. Sometimes the Gatekeeper appears in a more enigmatic or mythic guise. I have met the Gatekeeper, in my dreams, as a slick fellow beckoning me toward an open archway leading to delightful vistas of life possibilities while holding shut a door I was trying to force open. I have met the Gatekeeper in dreams — and on the dashboard of an Indian taxi driver after riding on Air India — as elephant-headed Ganesh, and as a black dog who sometimes walks on two legs, as Anubis does.

The Gatekeeper can be a trickster, especially if we are too set in our ways. On the roads of life, I am constantly alert to the shifting manifestations of this archetype, especially at airports while on the way to a different plane. At the Seattle airport, a cute, dark-skinned TSA agent laughed in my face when she inspected my driver's license. "Why are you laughing?" I asked her. "It's because of your name. In my language, 'Moss' means 'banana.'" "What language would that be?" "Somali." The humorous side of the Gatekeeper was definitely in play that day. Just think about it. Being teased at an American airport because your name means something funny in *Somali.*

Many years ago, after I sent my carry-ons through the X-ray machine at my home airport, I was stopped by the security guards. "You got a lampshade in here?" The guard indicated my drum bag. "Actually, it's a drum." I willingly extracted the simple frame drum that has powered many, many group journeys in my workshops, so they could see. "Will you play it for us?" the guard requested. "Excuse me?" "Go on, we'd like you to play." So there, just inside the security barrier, I was tapping out the heartbeat of the drum, surrounded by smiling faces. That felt like another good start to the day.

I've saved the best story about a brush with the airport Gatekeeper for last. I had been leading a shamanic gathering on a very special mountain and had rushed to the airport without considering what tools and toys I had stuffed in my drum bag. On the other side of the X-ray machine, a security guard asked me, "Is this yours?" To my horror, I saw he was holding up a ceremonial Lakota knife with an elk-bone handle that he had just removed from my drum bag. He extracted the nine-inch blade from the sheath and held it up. "Wait here. I have to get my supervisor."

Wild thoughts were thrashing in my brain. They'll arrest me. They'll grill me. At least they'll give me a tongue-lashing for being such a fool as to leave that knife in my carry-ons.

The supervisor appeared. His first words were: "What time is your flight?"

"Six fifteen."

"Good. We've got time to get this in your checked luggage so it can meet you at the other end. I'll walk you back to the ticket desk." With this, he handed me the knife, still out of its sheath.

I wondered if I was dreaming as I accompanied him, knife in hand, back through security.

"Go on, do it," he said.

"Do what?"

"You're Australian, aren't you? Do the Crocodile Dundee thing."

So I put on my best Strine accent and snarled, brandishing the knife, "Call that a knife? *This* is a bloody knife, mate!"

Gales of laughter. The ticket agent was delighted to put his long line of passengers on hold while he dashed to get my knife into my checked suitcase, saying, "I know you Aussies can't go anywhere without a bloody knife." I guess the Gatekeeper was truly in laughing mood that day. And that he sometimes makes special rules for people from Down Under.

14

Symbol Magnets

We all have certain electric and magnetic powers within us[,] and ourselves exercise an attractive and repelling force, according as we come into touch with something like or unlike.

— GOETHE, IN J. P. ECKERMANN, *Conversations with Goethe*

When Jung was immersed in his study of the symbolism of the fish in Christianity, alchemy, and world mythology, the theme started leaping at him in everyday life. On April 1, 1949, he made some notes about an ancient inscription describing a man whose bottom half was a fish. At lunch that day, he was served fish. In the conversation, there was talk of the custom of making an "April fish" — a European term for "April fool" — of someone. In the afternoon, a former patient of Jung's, whom he had not seen for months, arrived at his house and showed him some "impressive" pictures of fish. That evening, Jung was shown embroidery that featured fishy sea monsters. The next day, another former patient he had not seen in a decade recounted a dream in which a large fish swam toward her.

Several months later, mulling over this sequence as an example of the phenomenon he dubbed synchronicity, Jung walked by the lake near his house, returning to the same spot several times. The last time he repeated this loop, he found a fish a foot long lying on top of the seawall.

Jung had seen no one else on the lakeshore that morning. While the fish might have been dropped by a bird, its appearance seemed to him quite magical, part of a "run of chance" in which more than "chance" seemed to be at play.[27]

If we're keeping count (as Jung did), this sequence includes six discrete instances of meaningful coincidence, five of them bobbing up, like koi in a pond, within twenty-four hours, and all reflecting Jung's preoccupation with the symbolism of the fish. Such unlikely riffs of coincidence prompted Jung to ask whether it is possible that the physical world mirrors psychic processes "as continuously as the psyche perceives the physical world." In her discussion of how inner and outer events can mirror each other, Jungian analyst Marie-Louise von Franz suggested that, "if the psychic mirrorings of the material world — in short, the natural sciences — really constitute valid statements about matter, then the reverse mirror-relation would also have to be valid. This would mean that *material events in the external world would have to be regarded as statements about conditions in the objective psyche.*"[28]

Some of the greatest minds of the past century — Jung, Wolfgang Pauli, and David Bohm — sought to model a universe in which mind and matter, subject and object, inner and outer, are everywhere interweaving. Events, both physical and psychic, unfold from a unified field, the *unus mundus* of the alchemists, that may be synonymous with Bohm's "implicate order." Their interaction escapes our ordinary perception of causation and of time and space. Jung said, "Precisely because the psychic and the physical are mutually dependent...they may be identical somewhere beyond our present experience."[29]

Living symbols deeply ingrained in the imaginal history of humankind are charged with magnetic force, which can draw clusters of events together. For those familiar with tarot, it feels at such moments as if one of the Greater Trumps — representing archetypal forces — is at play in the world. Traditional diviners understand this, as do true priests and priestesses. Thus one of the Odu, or patterns, of Ifa, the oracle of the Yoruba, is held to bring the fierce orisha Ogun into the space, while another is believed to carry spirits of the dead into the realm of the living.

When that happens, you don't just study the pattern; you move to accommodate or propitiate the power that is manifesting.

To grasp the full power of a symbol, we need to go back to the root meaning of the word. *Symbol* is derived from the Greek σύμβολον (*sýmbolon*), which combines συν- (syn-), meaning "together," and βολή (bolē), a "throw" or a "cast." A symbol is that which is "thrown together" or "cast together." This is very close to the root meaning of *coincidence*. In Latin, to coincide is to "fall together." So it's not surprising that, when symbols are in play, coincidence multiplies. The first literary mention of a symbol is in the Homeric Hymn to Hermes, in which the god Hermes exclaims on finding a tortoise, "O what a happy symbol for me," before turning the tortoise shell into a lyre. In the ancient world, *sýmbolon* came to mean a "token," that which brings things together. Thus a symbol might be a pair of tokens that could be fitted together to make a single object. Such tokens might be broken halves of a potsherd, a ring, or a seal. They would vouch for the truthfulness of a messenger, or an enduring loyalty.

The magnetic power of a symbol in our lives can bring together inner and outer events in ways that shift our perception of reality. We learn best about these things through direct experience and through stories — like Jung's fish tale — that we can trust.

Antlered Synchronicity

Several years ago, I immersed myself in the study of a symbol that is as important in religion and mythology as that of the fish: the symbol of the antlered deer. I found that in many ancient and indigenous traditions, antlers are a symbol of spiritual authority because they grow above the physical head, reaching toward the realm of spirit. They signify regeneration because they die and grow back bigger than before. They are worn by Cernunnos, the ancient Celtic master of the animals; by Mongol women shamans; and by the *rotiyaner*, or "men of good minds," the traditional chiefs of the Six Nations of the Longhouse, or Iroquois. Visually, deer antlers suggest the shape of a tree, even the World Tree that shamans climb; the resemblance is in the French word for antlers, which are called the *bois* — wood — of the deer. There is a mystical connection between the deer, especially the flying deer (*cerf volant*) and the early kings of France.[30]

Studying religious iconography in France in 2005, I became fascinated by the moment in the history of the Western imagination when the old pagan image of the Antlered One fused with that of the Christ. You can view the results on the facade of the great Gothic church of Saint-Eustache at Les Halles, once the site of the famous market. Look up near the top and you'll find, lording it over the gargoyles, the figure of an antlered stag with the Calvary cross between his antlers. According to legend, Saint Eustace (to give him the Anglo version of his name) was formerly a pagan Roman general named Placidus, who reveled in the hunt until, one day, he confronted a magnificent stag through whose deep eyes the Christ light shone. Christ spoke to him through the deer. The general gave up hunting and converted to the new religion. This moment of conversion through the agency of the deer has been memorialized in numerous painted and woven and sculpted images, including a marvelous fifteenth-century painting by Pisanello that I viewed in the National Gallery in London.

The Saint Eustace legend may be an invention designed to claim the luster of a commanding symbol of the old ways for the new religion, just as churches were placed on the sacred sites where pre-Christian rituals had been celebrated. However, the theme of the power of the deer spirit to tame the killer in man resonated with me deeply, because on a mountain in the Adirondacks of New York, I had heard a similar tale from mountain men who knew nothing of Placidus or Eustace: that three hunters, on separate occasions, had come face-to-face with a great stag in that wild terrain, and that each time, something in the deep, steady eyes of the deer had persuaded the hunter to lay down his rifle and go home.

Not long after that trip to France, I was talking on my cell phone about the theme of Christ in the stag while walking my dog in a park in upstate New York that is notably clean. As I described the stag with the cross between his antlers on the church at Les Halles, I glanced down and saw an orange cardboard disk at my feet. It bore the image of a stag with a Calvary cross shining between his antlers. This was one of those moments when the universe gets personal. I knew that, in that moment, the symbol blazing in my mind was shining back at me on the grass at my feet.

I put the cardboard disk in my wallet and have carried it ever since, a token from the world. I did not identify the source of this version of the stag with the cross until, on my way to give a talk at a bookshop in Vancouver, B.C., some months later, I stopped at an Irish pub across the street. I needed to use what Canadians call the washroom, and as I did what boys do, I saw the image from the cardboard disk in front of my nose, in a framed poster for Jägermeister, an herbal liqueur whose name means "hunt-master" and that (I later learned from my youngest daughter) is a favorite on college campuses with kids who want to get "hammered."

Jung noted in his foreword to his most important work on synchronicity that "my researches into the history of symbols, and of the fish symbol in particular, brought the problem [of explaining synchronicity] ever closer to me."[31] His experiences of symbols irrupting into the physical world led him to sympathize with Goethe's magical view, noted in the chapter epigraph, that "we all have certain electric and magnetic powers within us[,] and ourselves exercise an attractive and repelling force, according as we come into touch with something like or unlike."[32] It seems likely that such powers are magnified when our minds and our environment are charged with the energy of a living symbol.

When our minds are charged with a living symbol, we sometimes seem to attract related events. And because a true symbol has autonomous power in the realm of the collective psyche, a symbol may burst into our ordinary reality. Earlier peoples spoke of these things in a simpler language, as the interplay between humans and gods, spirits, and elemental powers of nature. I confess to having sympathy for the older way of understanding, as did Jung, who invented the terms *archetype* and *psychoid* and *collective unconscious* in an effort to define these phenomena in a vocabulary acceptable to the modern scientific mind, yet loved to quote the old Latin tag *Omnia plena diis esse* (All things are full of gods).

Following is another personal example of a symbol irrupting into my life in a way that felt like the intervention of a power from the world-behind-the-world.

The Odin Squirt and the Fox Girl

The following three incidents played out over three weeks in early 2005, and I recorded them in my journals.

First, I was called to work with a Danish man who had been physically crippled by a complex of diseases he developed after severe mercury poisoning. The collapse of his health contributed to the collapse of his marriage. Cynical, misogynist, reclusive — and fixedly atheistic, denying the existence of the soul — he eventually sought to end his pain with a bottle of sleeping pills.

He needed a soul guide, and I made it my intention to call in a guide he could perceive and trust and believe in. Instantly Odin appeared in a wide-brimmed hat and a flying garment, swinging a staff, with his ravens flapping about him. The figure of Odin was vivid and an entirely spontaneous revelation. His back was turned to me because all his attention was on the suicide. The Dane had no hesitation in accepting Odin as his guide. Odin took him, not to any of the realms of the Aesir, but deep into the body of a primal goddess under the waves. I was deeply moved to see this man's healing and rehab begin in the deeps of the Divine Feminine through a gate opened by one-eyed Odin.

Interesting, on the mythic plane, that the man's problems flowed from a toxic relationship with Mercury. The Romans identified Odin with Mercury. "Above all gods they worship Mercury, and count it no sin to win his favor on certain days by human sacrifice," wrote Tacitus. It seemed the man who had suffered from mercury poisoning had healed his relationship with Mercury.

A week later, I met an editor for dinner at a seafood restaurant. During the meal he stabbed a lemon slice with a fork to season his fish — and shot a jet of lemon juice into my left eye, temporarily blinding me. He did not notice what happened.

I said, dabbing my eye with a napkin, "I wonder what it means when a supposedly friendly editor blinds you in the left eye."

After a quick apology, he shot back without losing a beat, "It's the price Odin paid to Mimir for his wisdom."

I was impressed that his mind had gone straight to the myth of how Odin gave up an eye in order to drink from the well of prophecy and remembrance. After a mouthful of fish, the editor told me that some larger force definitely must have been at work with the lemon squirt, since he was trained to manage such things in a way that few of us are. "I know how to use a fork. I was trained as a sous-chef in Paris to get this kind of thing exactly right. I could not have shot you in the eye unless some powerful force was orchestrating this, a force such as Odin."

A week after the Odin squirt, I was on a plane bound to Minneapolis on the first leg of a transcontinental journey. The flight attendant seemed to have stepped out of the Otherworld. She was milk white with reddish hair and moved like a fleet little woodland animal. I decided she might be an arctic fox — or the altered astral form of a fox, a fox's attempt to project a human double. When she served drinks, I noticed that her left eye was brown while her right eye was blue. I told her she had magical eyes and looked like she had just come from the realm of Faerie.

It's said that, if your eyes are of different colors, it can mean they see into different worlds. This is a milder version of the Odin motif, where the seer loses one of his physical eyes — part of his ordinary vision — as the price of vision into the deeper world.

How do you develop your own sense of the symbols that have magnetism for you? Watch how *life rhymes*. Track correspondences between the images that are playing in your mind, in your dreams, in the books you read, and in the movies you watch, and what pops up in the world around you. Since humans are forgetful, it's essential to note these themes in your journal as they repeat and evolve over time.

Try this game: choose a finite interval of time (a lunch break, for example, or the evening commute, or half an hour in the woods) and notice and record *three things* that enter your field of perception during this period.

If you have a question or theme on your mind, you may find that the three things you observe provide guidance, even a very direct message. But this game is less about putting your question to the world than about letting the world speak to you. It's about developing pattern recognition and field perception.

As you go on playing the game, you'll grow your self-awareness in interesting ways. You'll become more aware of which are your primary senses. If you find that, like me, you are highly visual, you may want to push yourself to do more with less active or dormant senses, making it your game to, for example, *smell* or *listen* to what is around you.

Most important, you'll enhance your ability to play witness to your everyday self. The ability to observe yourself from a witness perspective and notice where you place your attention and how you choose what you'll focus on in a day is crucial to the art of conscious living.

In this way, we grow the poetic consciousness that allows us to taste and touch what rhymes and resonates in the world we inhabit, and to come alive to how the world-behind-the-world reveals itself by fluttering the veils of our consensual reality.

15

Life as a Conscious Dream

The world is a vast dream, dreamed by a single being, but in such a way that all the dream characters dream too. Hence, everything interacts and harmonizes with everything else.

—— SCHOPENHAUER

I often read a page or two of Emerson before greeting the sun. For me, he is the wisest of American philosophers and the most practical, because his words create a stir in the spirit that is a wonderful incitement to *action*. He is the perennial enemy of hand-me-down systems of belief and self-limiting notions about what is possible in a life. When we are wandering lost in a fog of confusion in the low marshlands of groupthink, he pipes the tune and shines the light that will get us back to the upward slopes of our life purpose.

Three Words from Emerson

The other day, while leading a five-day adventure in Active Dreaming at the Omega Institute, I guided a group of brave and ready souls on a journey to a real place in the imaginal realm that I call the House of Time. It is the kind of locale that creators, shamans, and mystics have always wanted to visit, a place where we may encounter an inner teacher who is the master of any field that compels our best attention and study, and where any book of secrets — even the Book of Life containing our sacred contract — may be accessible. If you would like to go there, you'll find detailed instructions in my book *Dreamgates*.

While drumming for the group to provide fuel and focus for the journey to the library in the House of Time, I found myself in contact with intelligences who have guided and inspired my work in the past. It seemed that Emerson, in high collar and frock coat, had joined the group. I do not say this was the individual spirit of the great sage; I do not claim the privilege of a personal interview, and I am sure that, wherever Emerson may now be, he has many things to do. I say only that for a few moments I seemed to be in the presence of a figure who embodied some essence of Emerson's thought. I was eager to receive insights I could easily retain, while my consciousness was working on several levels, including that of drumming for the members of the group and watching over their adventures.

My Emerson gave me three words: *Rectitude. Plenitude. Attitude.* The following morning in the twilight before dawn, as the first pink suffused the gray sky, I tracked these clues through Emerson's essays and letters and through the pedigrees of the terms themselves.

Rectitude

In its origin, rectitude is the virtue of being straight, or upright, in your conduct and condition. It derives from the Latin *rectus*, or "straight." It has nothing to do with a narrow moralism. As Emerson wields this word, it is the property and armor of the brave soul who dares to live by his own lights. In his famous 1838 address to Harvard Divinity School — a speech the faculty tried to suppress but the senior class insisted upon — Emerson defined "the grand strokes of rectitude" as "a bold benevolence" and as the independence of mind that enables us to ignore the counsel and caution of our friends when they seek to hold us back from pursuing our calling, and the readiness to follow that calling without concern for praise or profit. Those who can do this, said Emerson, are "the Imperial Guard of Virtue" and "the heart and soul of nature." They "rise refreshed on hearing a threat"; they come to a crisis "graceful and beloved as a bride"; "they can say like Napoleon at Massena that they were not themselves until the battle began to go against them."

Plenitude

Plenitude is fullness or abundance, and the word comes from the Latin *plenus*, or "full." For Emerson, plenitude — abundance — is our natural condition, and we lack it only when we fail to live from the fullness and integrity of our own spirit. When we develop self-trust, we gain "the plenitude of its energy and power to repair harms," he instructs in his essay "Heroism." "There is no limit to the Resources of Man," he adds in a letter on that theme. "The one fact that shines through all this plenitude of powers is...that the world belongs to the energetic, belongs to the wise."

Attitude

Attitude has an even more suggestive etymology. It first came into usage to describe the posture that an actor playing a role strikes on the stage. If we go farther back, we find it is a kissing cousin of the word *aptitude*, and both share the Latin root *aptus*, which means "fit" or "suited" — in short, ready for something. Our attitudes indeed determine what experiences we are apt to encounter on our roads of life. "The healthy attitude of human nature," Emerson instructs us in his essay "Self-Reliance," is "the nonchalance of boys who are sure of a dinner" — in other words, the confidence that the universe will support us. In the face of hardship and challenge, we need to strike the posture of determination that, "by [its] very attitude and...tone of voice, puts a stop to defeat," Emerson adds in a letter on his essay "Resources."

We are now entering one of the great open secrets of life: "We are magnets in an iron globe," as Emerson told the young men at Harvard. "We have keys to all doors....The world is all gates, all opportunities, strings of tension waiting to be struck." We choose which doors will open or remain closed. We decide what we will attract or repel in life, according to whether we are straight, and full, and ready.

Ten Noncommandments for Conscious Living

On the day I sat down to complete this chapter, I noticed a car parked on my block with a decal in the shape of twin tablets on the driver's side door. I confirmed my suspicion that the car owner had placed the Ten Commandments there. As I noted earlier, one of my everyday synchronicity games is to pay attention to what the first unusual thing I spot in the street might be saying to me. The Ten Commandments on the driver's side door got me thinking about framing this chapter as a list of suggested personal commandments for conscious living. I decided not to go that way, partly because the precepts I want to suggest cannot be set in stone, being forever open to change and fresh discovery, and most especially for a reason I'll get to at the end. So here we go with ten suggestions for conscious living, beyond tracking the Synchron-O-city Beast. I haven't numbered them, because you are free to shuffle them in any way, or add to the list, or, best of all, make your own list.

Make Every Day Thanksgiving

If the only prayer you said in your life was "Thank you," that would suffice. The counsel is from Meister Eckhart, the medieval German theologian and mystic. It is my own philosophy of prayer, and it is the practice of people who live close to the earth, as well as to the heavens, and give thanks daily for its gifts.

In the United States, where I now live, Thanksgiving is an all-American holiday I generally enjoy, though it was completely foreign in the country where I grew up. At Thanksgiving, I rarely think about the Pilgrim fathers getting through a rough winter with the help of red people who did not yet understand what the irruption of pink people on this continent would mean for them. But I often think about how, for the First Peoples of America, prayer is often a practice of returning thanks for life and all that supports life in our conscious, interconnected universe, and how this is not just part of one big turkey day but an everyday affirmation.

Here's a simple affirmation that came to me long ago when my dreams and visions drew me into the imaginal realm of a Native American people — the Haudenosaunee, or Iroquois — for whom returning thanks is part of what keeps the world turning:

I return thanks for the gifts of this lifetime
and for its challenges.
I seek to walk in balance between earth and sky,
affirming.

Play First, Work Later

Let's review what happened in the Laetoli Valley in Tanzania in 1976, when a couple of young archaeologists in a team led by Mary Leakey were horsing around with dried clumps of elephant dung. Ducking a flying pellet, Andrew Hill found himself prone above three sets of footprints. Closer inspection proved that they had been preserved in volcanic ash, hardened by rain to a cementlike consistency, at least 3.6 million years ago. The way the big toes were set parallel to the others and the evidence of a "heel first" mode of walking indicated that the prints had been left by protohumans rather than apes. Mary Leakey was moved by the discovery that the female in the trio had paused in her journey to look toward the left — perhaps to check on the child who was walking in her steps, or to scan for danger, which might include the plume of an active volcano.

So many great discoveries have their origin in play. The best work is done in a spirit of play. This requires us to forget the consequences and do what we are doing for its own sake. You may not find the Laetoli footprints, now regarded as one of the greatest discoveries in the history of archaeology, every time you fool around with elephant dung — but, hey, it's odor-free and (when nicely dried) a great substitute for a beach ball.

Play at Work, Work at Play

Riding on Southwest Airlines, I am seated next to a pleasant woman who asks the young male flight attendant for hot tea. He amazes her by bringing a selection of gourmet Stash tea bags along with the standard Earl Gray and chamomile.

"Southwest carries Stash teas? That's amazing."

"Oh, no," says the attendant. "I borrow them from our airline hotels because I think passengers deserve a better selection."

That flight attendant got full marks from me for turning his job into a game, in which he makes it his pleasure to go the extra mile — or in this case, the extra tea bag — for the sheer joy of seeing the effect this has on people. He is a model of a cardinal principle of conscious living: when you can't turn your play into your work, turn your work into play.

Yeah, right, but what if you're in a job you don't like, but you can't walk out because there are bills to pay and kids to get through school and it's a cold world out there?

Can't you still learn from the flight attendant with the stash of tea bags? Your employer may be less good-humored than Southwest seems to be (I'm told they run a smile check on would-be employees), but you could still make it your game to commit one random act of kindness or creativity any day at the workplace. If you try that, don't burden what you do with expectations of any reward or even any particular response; just do something nice or fun and enjoy doing it for its own sake. Be where you are and make the most of it. Don't make work even worse than it is by putting down your present situation and investing your energy in wishing you were somewhere else — until you are ready to make the move and go somewhere else.

Maybe your work situation is so bad that you can't even risk bringing smiles and flowers to the office. Then you may want to consider other creative strategies for making the best of your day. One of my favorites is what I call the revenge novel.

A friend of mine, a brilliant scientist, was researching a new generation of medical technology at one of the country's leading hospitals. The project was important and challenging, but the human situation was toxic. Her days were blighted by a despotic, self-absorbed project director whom my friend referred to as The Vampiress. Colleagues were distracted by endless politics and infighting. Coauthors of studies did not appreciate my friend's vastly superior command of the English language or her wicked sense of irony. She would find herself utterly drained as she fought the subway system on her evening commute.

For light relief, she started making word pictures of incidents from the office in a series of emails to me. I found these quite dazzling and devilishly funny. I called her and said, "If I were you, I would look at each day on the job as a glorious opportunity to gather fresh material for my great revenge novel, the one in which I'll settle accounts with The Vampiress, the Bottlenose Plagiarist, and all the other characters who've been making my workdays a misery." She loved the idea. She started collecting her sketches in a folder and was halfway through a draft of a novel by the time she was transferred out of the domain of The Vampiress. She was almost sorry to go, since she was now having so much fun treating every day on the job as a literary raid.

Writing a novel may not be your game, but there are all sorts of variants on this approach. Another friend made up a soap opera about her colleagues, not writing anything down but regaling trusted friends — including a few from the office — with successive installments. Since I was an occasional visitor at her company, I got a guest role, though I heard about this only years later. She cast Anthony Quinn to play me. Not so bad.

Courage Is Fear Conquered by Love

I saw this message once on a board outside a church while I was trying to come up with the right thing to say to a friend who seemed to me to be paralyzed by fear in confronting a work situation. I passed along the message, which I believe is excellent counsel.

The point is that courageousness is different from fearlessness. If you are fearless, you may be merely crazy, or reckless, or lacking in imagination. Courage is the ability to go through fear because you are driven by something that is stronger than fear. Courage is a quality of the heart; you won't find it anywhere else. The French word for heart — *coeur* — is in there.

When you are gripped by fear in the face of an experience that will take you beyond your comfort zone, you may be at a point of supreme opportunity. You can either break down or break through.

When we take greater risks, we draw the support of greater powers.

Don't Block the River

The ancient Egyptians were rehearsed to make a "negative confession" in the Hall of Osiris on the other side of death. Among the many not-guilty statements they were coached to make in order to establish their right to move on to a happy afterlife was one that seems especially strange to us: "I have not obstructed water when it should flow." This made practical sense in a dry country where people's survival depended on catching the waters from the annual rising of a single river. It also makes great sense in the pattern of a life; we must not block the river, though we may seek to influence its course.

The Tewa Pueblo word for creativity or art is *po-wa-ha*. The three syllables mean "water-wind-breath." The understanding is that creating is a process of connecting to natural flow. The Tewa do not have a separate word for art because they do not experience art as an activity separate from any other in life. Creativity is as close as breathing; it is the spirit of life moving effortlessly through its cycles. *Po-wa-ha* is the energy that flows from everybody and everything…from the very source of life.[33]

David Whyte writes about the performance of a craftsman whose speed in accomplishing his work flawlessly seemed to lie in something other than merely pushing forward by willing it. The key, he says, is "a felt perception of the larger pattern" combined with "a restful yet attentive presence in the midst of our work" and the ability to draw on "some source of energy other than our constant applications of effort and will." It is surely true that, "if we attempt to engage the will continually, it exhausts us and prevents us from creating something with a pattern that endures."[34]

Don't Live in Other People's Boxes

"If you haven't the strength to impose your own terms upon life," as T. S. Eliot counseled, "you must accept the terms it offers you." This requires us to withhold our consent when anyone offers us a version of reality that is less than generous and that is not open to fresh possibilities.

I had occasion to think about this in a rather genial context when I ran into one of my favorite used-book dealers opening his store very early while I was out walking my dogs. I asked, hopefully, if he had a new consignment of books. No, he explained, his building had sprung some leaks, and he was there to wait for the plumbers. "Everything wears out," he declared, "including the brain."

I did not feel obliged to quarrel with this statement. As the owner of an old house, I know that certainly old plumbing wears out and old roofs spring leaks. Yet I was not going to endorse the notion that *everything* wears out, even if this appears to conform to the second law of thermodynamics as well as to much of our everyday experience. Neuroscience instructs us that brain cells can grow back, and that the neuroplasticity of the brain is so extraordinary that survivors of serious strokes can actually transfer functions from damaged areas to other parts. Of course, if you don't want your brain to wear out, you'd better use it!

I didn't endorse the statement that everything, including the brain, wears out, and I didn't deny it. I simply withheld my consent and adopted the agnostic position on the matter. There are many occasions when it's rather more important to take this stance — for example, when someone asks us to agree to the proposition that "you can't trust people" or "there'll never be enough to go around," or pushes the bumper sticker philosophy that "shit happens."

We are not required to argue or to preach when we withhold our consent from opinions and mind-sets that turn our inhabited world into a box. We simply decline to join others inside their mind-made boxes while we proceed to develop and impose our own terms on the world we inhabit.

To succeed in that, we not only need to go around other people's mind traps but also need to drop our own negative mantras. I'm fierce about that, as a teacher. When I hear anyone in one of my workshops committing a negative mantra (which may begin "I'm no good at…" or "I've never been able to…"), I ask her to go outside and spit that thought out on the ground. Fair's fair. I tell my groups that if they ever catch me committing a negative mantra of my own, they can send me out of the room to do the same thing.

When It's Jump Time, Jump

In Greek, there are two kinds of time. *Chronos* time is what we observe when we look at a clock and measure out our days. *Kairos* time doesn't operate at a tick-tock pace. It is the "appointed time," when powers and movements of a deeper world irrupt into our regular lives, when the Greater Trumps are in play.

It is a risky time, offering both opportunity and danger and the excitement of living on the edge. Jean Houston calls it "Jump Time."[35] Lyanda Lynn Haupt says beautifully, in *Crow Planet*: "It is a time brimming with meaning, a time more potent than 'normal' time."[36]

The celebrated Greek sculptor Lysippos carved Kairos in stone as a winged figure with a razor and hair hanging down over his face. In words attributed by Poseidippos to Kairos himself, the razor is a sign to men that Kairos is sharper than any sharp edge. Kairos's hair hangs over his face to signal that "he who meets me must take me by the forelock." The back of his head is bald because "once I have sped by none can seize me from behind." It is Jump Time in our world, as well as in our lives.

To quote Lyanda Haupt again, we live in a time "when our collective actions over the next several years will decide whether earthly life will continue its descent into ecological ruin and death or flourish in beauty and diversity."[37]

Look Up

In the Mohawk language, which my dreams required me to study, if I want to say to you, "Don't forget," I will say: "Tohsa sasa nikonh'ren." This expression literally means "Do not let your mind fall." The fuller meaning is: Do not let your mind fall from the Earth-in-the-Sky, the higher world from which Sky Woman came to dance our Earth into being, the world-beyond-the-world that holds the origin and meaning of human endeavors. The traditional teaching of the Six Nations of the Longhouse, of which the Mohawk people is one, is that when men let their minds fall, our world falls into the Dark Times.

All of which could be summed up by the phrase *Look up.*

Don't Do Anything Serious without Your Sense of Humor

It's vital to identify what makes each of us lighten up and want to stay on this good earth, and to do as much of that as we possibly can. Maybe the appropriate care is an emergency delivery of bubble bath, or a "Hello Kitty" vanity set (yes, to a grown-up daughter), or a movie date, or a glass of chardonnay, or peach cobbler, or a walk (in due season) on the beach or in the woods.

The best help is what makes us laugh and start to play life as a game again. Laughter is a sovereign healer and life preserver. Laughter that is convulsively rich and life renewing doesn't come from stand-up comics and hand-me-down jokes. It comes out of the deep, organic humus of life, out of spontaneous play. Sometimes this kind of laughter rises up from a chasm of pain and grief, even tragedy, and brings healing.

Absent fresh material or someone to play with, we can always pull up a clip from our inner archive of Funniest Home Videos. I sometimes think of the TSA guard who told me my name means "banana" in Somali. Or of the fellow who emailed me to tell me he wanted to follow a spiritual path but needed to put money in the bank first — so would I please dream the winning number in the upcoming Florida state lottery and send it to him.

There Is One Direction in Which All Space Is Open to Us

The sun rises from behind the mountains, and golden light bursts over the lake. Though the analogy is too pedestrian for the glory of this moment, it seems to me that an immense lightbulb has come on, impossible to miss yet difficult to look at head-on.

The moment before I walked barefoot across the wet grass to wait for the sun by the shore, I was rereading lines from Emerson that give exact shape to the sense of illumination and direction that is now with me:

> Each man has his own vocation. The talent is the call. There is one direction in which all space is open to him. He has faculties silently inviting him thither to endless exertion. He is like a ship in a river; he runs against obstructions on every side but one; on that side all obstruction is taken away, and he sweeps serenely over a deepening channel into an infinite sea.
>
> This talent and this call depend on his organization, or the mode in which the general soul incarnates itself in him. He inclines to do something which is easy to him, and good when it is

done, but which no other man can do. He has no rival. For the more truly he consults his own powers, the more difference will his work exhibit from the work of any other. His ambition is exactly proportioned to his powers. The height of the pinnacle is determined by the breadth of the base. Every man has this call of the power to do somewhat unique, and no man has any other call.[38]

This passage, from Emerson's "Spiritual Laws," gives vital navigational guidance for our life journeys. Every word is as precise as a compass bearing. To read this passage deeply and take it to heart is to turn on the light in a darkened room or put the sun in the sky.

The talent is the call. When we follow our soul's calling and give ourselves to *the* work, the life Work that is ours and no other's, our gifts are multiplied, because we draw to ourselves supporting powers from the unseen, starting with our own creative genius.

There is one direction in which all space is open to us. This explains why, when we are unsure of or uncommitted to our calling, we find blocks and opposition placed in our paths, doors slammed in our faces, savage reversals of fortune or of health that compel us to ask what we are doing in our lives. Such obstruction isn't random, and it's about more than toughening us up. Dead ends and adversity, repeated often enough, can make us aware that we've been following the wrong charts. Knowing that we have been misdirected gives us the chance to find our true direction.

On that side all obstruction is taken away. When we follow the soul's direction, the way ahead is open, and wind and water flow with us. We "sweep serenely over a deepening channel into an infinite sea." We draw new allies, events, and resources to us. Chance encounters and benign coincidence support us and ease our passage in ways that are inexplicable to those from whom the spiritual laws of human existence are hidden.

What we now deliver in our world is unique, yet it springs from *the mode in which the general soul incarnates itself in us.* We draw from "that age-long memoried self that shapes the elaborate shell of the mollusc and the child in the womb, that teaches the birds to make their nest," as Yeats wrote, thrillingly, in *The Trembling of the Veil*. The poet added that "genius is a crisis that joins that buried self for certain moments to our trivial daily mind." Yes, but Emerson arouses us to the understanding that the flash of genius can become a steady beacon for a voyage in which the mixed crew of personalities that compose the self are willing to work the ropes together because the helmsman is unerring.

We have no rival when we follow our one direction and live as creators. To be a creator is to bring something new into the world, the thing only we can give.

Each of us has this call of the power to do something unique, and no one has any other call. Ah. As I write this line, releasing it from gender to become fully the property of all, the sun calls me, laying a path of light clear across the inland sea and through my window so that it shines before me. My pencil, on the table, glows in this brilliant morning light, *silently inviting me to endless exertion* with the talent I am given, the kind of exertion that is no sweat because it is the soul's delight.

The Sole Commandment of Conscious Living

Carpe diem, goes the old Latin tag. "Seize the day." The sole commandment of conscious living is no less proactive, but more conscious: *Choose the day.*

We have learned that what we encounter on any day has a great deal to do with what we bring to that day. We draw or repel different events and encounters according to our attitudes and the basic energy we are carrying. We find doors open or closed according to our willingness or refusal to change our expectations and our plans as circumstances change.

We choose every day, whether we are aware of this or not. If we tell ourselves we have no choice, that is a choice we are making. If we tell ourselves we have no choice because a situation is beyond our control, we forget that we can still choose our response to the world, and this can change everything. Whenever I hear someone — perhaps a voice within myself — bleating or protesting that the world is cruel and can't be changed, I think of Viktor Frankl in the nightmare of Auschwitz.

At the close of a beautiful week of soul healing and shared dreaming on Cortes Island, I asked the members of our circle to choose the day in a personal statement. Here's a sampling of what they said:

I choose to be present today with all of my senses.

I choose to have Tiger in my heart.

I choose to follow my soul's purpose.

I choose to see my waking life as a dream.

I choose to travel with the energy of the group.

I choose to be compassionate.

I choose to be a survivor.

I choose to soar with the bird and see my roads from a higher perspective.

I choose the fire.

My own statement on that day: "I choose to live as if everything matters."

Truth, in our lives, is what we remember and act upon. Lists of rules or intentions can become like grocery lists; we are forever in danger of forgetting items or getting what matters mixed up. So my list of personal commandments reduces to this: *Choose the day*. The content of that choice is less important than the consciousness that we have a choice and need to approach life, on any day, as *choosers*, not spectators, victims, or consumers. This is how we get to the Place of the Lion.

The Place of the Lion

You are at a zoo on a Sunday afternoon. People are wandering about, snacking and chatting as they inspect the birds and other animals. As you approach the big-cat enclosures, you are uneasy because you know that big cats don't belong in confinement.

When you come to the lion pen, you are disgusted because people are mocking the great beast, pulling faces — until someone screams that the gate is open and the lion could get them. Now all the people are running away.

Instead of fleeing, you step through the open gate into the Place of the Lion. The great beast runs toward you and leaps up...and his great paws are on your shoulders...and he licks your face like a friendly dog. He wills you to turn around and look at the scene in the zoo in order to understand what is really going on here.

When you look back, you see that it is the *humans* who are living in cages. In the comfort of their suburban houses and malls and supermarkets, they have failed to notice that they have walled themselves into places of confinement. When you look beyond the lion, you see there are no walls, only an open horizon of wild freedom and possibility. The lion says to you, in his gravely lion voice, "You see, my dear, humans are the only animals who *choose* to live in cages."

I have taken a *big* dream of my own and made it yours. As we've seen, this is something active dreamers can learn to do for one another. We can do this for a person in need, or a friend, or a small group, or — as we are about to see — a whole community.

PART 3

Toward a Commonwealth
of Dreamers

We must bring our true selves into the world....
The psychic starvation brought about by removing soul
from the world produces insatiable greed, for when the world
is no longer surrounded with soul a vast emptiness
intervenes that must be filled.

— ROBERT SARDELLO,
Facing the World with Soul

16

Cry of the Trees

Trees are poems that Earth writes upon the sky.
—— KAHLIL GIBRAN

I am conscious of the dance of trees when I am in the evergreen forests of the Pacific Northwest and the red cedars shake their frills like
belles at an old-time ball. Or when the madronas, yearning toward the
ocean, roll back their outer bark to reveal the green of an avocado that
has taken off its skin. All that summer week at one of my trainings at
Mosswood Hollow in the foothills of the Cascades, we delighted in a
world of green: frilly greens of the cedars, mossy greens hanging from
high trunks and draping stumps and nurse logs, bottle-green shadows
of the deep woods, juicy greens of berry bushes and young vines, splashy
brown-greens of the beaver swamp.

On our last morning, preparing for an exercise in community visioning, I asked the members of our circle to join hands and imagine
that we were creating a dream tree with our joined energies: "Let your
awareness go down to the souls of your feet. You feel yourself standing
with the earth. You are reaching down now, through the souls of your
feet. You are reaching deep into the earth, going deep and spreading

wide, as the roots of a tree go deep and spread wide. You feel your energy filaments touching and clasping the energy roots of all of us in this circle. We are coming together, forming a root-ball deep within the earth. As you breathe in, feel the earth energy rising up to form the trunk of our dream tree — our One Tree, soaring toward the sky, spreading its canopy to catch the light. Now we are feeding on sun fire…"

In this way, we wove our energies together in a dream tree that we intended to use as a base for visioning, from which we could scout in different directions to fulfill a common agenda: to find new ways to bring dreaming into our environments and communities all over the map. I suggested that, during the drumming, we would all find our way to an observation deck or tree house high in the upper branches of the dream tree. We could look out from there to see what we needed to see, zoom in on things we needed to study closely, or take flight like birds to visit places many looks away.

When I started the drumming, the energy form of the One Tree emerged vividly. I could feel it, see it, smell it. It was unlike any previous tree of vision I have used. It was an immense elder of the rain forest, as wide and tall as a skyscraper. Its lower trunk was alive with creeping and slithering things, including thousands of snakes, hard to tell apart from the creepers and strangler vines until they darted out.

I moved gingerly to a shelflike space in the tree high above, where a giant white heron was perched looking out over vast distances. I shot out from there to meet one elder tree after another — a great Douglas fir, an ancient oak, a mighty poplar, a wide banyan rooting itself again and again from its branches. They showed me scenes of pain and destruction in the landscapes they inhabit. I was made to watch clear-cutting in the evergreen forests of the Pacific Northwest, and to be present during brutal deforestation in Brazil, with great machines rending the earth, and the stink of smoke and the cries of dying trees everywhere. The grief of the trees entered my being. It was like being made to witness the rape and butchery of innocents. Choking and sobbing, I had difficulty sustaining the beat of the drum.

I heard the voices of the tree elders. Their message, in different accents, was the same.

You use trees for your dreaming.

The trees need humans to dream with them.

The trees are dying because of the ignorance and greed of men,

and with them your world.

We need Tree Speakers to speak for the green world.

It is your duty to find them and give them voice and vision.

I received a vision from a great grove of elder trees native to many different regions, grouped in a council circle, with a human Speaker for each. I was drawn to an immense red cedar, its trunk at least sixty feet across and rising hundreds of feet toward the sky, and was told that this tree — over a thousand years old — still stands somewhere in the Pacific Northwest.

I saw and sensed more somber things. I smelled wood smoke during my own meditation. This was not the pleasant smoke of a wood fire, but the choking smoke of a forest going down. I received from the tree mind an image of the human species as a single body engaged in burning and destroying its own lungs, chain-smoking cigarettes that (in the vision) were actually burning or smoldering tree trunks.

That would make an arresting image for groups devoted to conserving the forests: a human who chain-smokes trees like cigarettes. It matches the data. In one year the "average" tree inhales twenty-six pounds of carbon dioxide (about the same amount exuded by the average car driven for eleven thousand miles) and exhales enough oxygen to keep a family of four breathing for twelve months.

I issued an invitation via every medium to which I had access for active dreamers everywhere to become Tree Speakers in a worldwide Grove of Dreamers:

Picture yourself standing with a great tree, joined hand to hand with all the dreamers in this forum, gently circling its trunk. Picture yourself putting down energy roots deep into the earth to join with the energies of other members of this community in a root-ball far beneath the surface.

Picture yourself gliding within or along the trunk of the great tree to an observation deck or tree house in the upper branches. This is your point of departure for the big journey. On that deck, you may be able to meet other active dreamers who are becoming Tree Speakers. You may travel from there, in whatever direction you are called, to enter the world of the trees, dream with the ancient ones of the forest, and learn what it means to be a Tree Speaker.

I believe that, seven generations beyond us, those who look back on our time will find that it was the cry of the trees that helped to restart the dreaming and foster the understanding that we must dream not only for ourselves but also for our communities and for all that shares life with us in our fragile bubble of air.

17

Dream Groups as Models
for a New Community

The real task of leadership is to confront people with their freedom.

— PETER BLOCK, *Community*

Community, as Peter Block defines it in a provocative book, is about the experience of belonging. To belong is to feel at home, to know you are among family or friends. When something belongs to you, you are an owner; you have a stake in something. Playing with the word, Block notes that *belonging* evokes longing to be — to come fully alive, to embody fully a deeper purpose in life.

The model leader in the kind of community Block seeks to midwife is one who can bring the right people together in the right way, name the right questions for group exploration ("What can we create together?"), and listen as others find their voices and their power. Such things are best done in small groups, which Block promotes as the best agents of transformation.

Active Dreaming groups are now at the vanguard in developing the kind of social space that Block advocates. Our dream groups are typically small (six to twelve people), and they establish a different kind of space and a deep sense of belonging to an intentional community. They are circles in which each member receives the gift of deep listening, the chance to play leader or teacher, and the opportunity to tell her life story and re-vision that story.

In Active Dreaming circles, we recognize the need for strong leadership to provide the structure and dynamic within which extraordinary group experiences can be shared. Leading includes selecting and defining a safe and protected physical space. It means gently insisting on time limits (dreamers can get things done on time), building and maintaining circle energy and keeping it moving for the two or three hours of a typical session, and making sure that everyone feels at home and that everyone's voice is heard. Part of the leader's job in an Active Dreaming circle is to ensure that a lively alternation of discussion, movement, and conscious group dream-travel keeps everyone alert and engaged.

Above all, the leader will enforce simple rules that make certain that no one present — least of all the leader herself — will try to claim authority over anyone else's dreams or life story. We are permitted only to comment on each other's material by saying, "If it were my dream" or "If it were my life." In this way, we offer associations and suggestions while encouraging the dreamer to claim the power of her own dreams — and to take the necessary action to embody their energy and guidance in the world. Finally, the leader of an Active Dreaming circle will give her power away repeatedly by inviting others to take charge in leading the processes.

In these ways, we fulfill Block's definition of the mode of leadership required to restore and re-story our communities: "Perhaps the real task of leadership is to confront people with their freedom."[39]

Creating and Maintaining an Active Dream Group

We need to share our dreams — our dreams from the night and our life dreams — with caring and supportive partners who can help us to unlock their meanings and bring their energy to heal and empower our everyday lives. An active dream group develops a wonderful energy of its own. Over the past fifteen years, Active Dreaming circles have sprung up all over the map, practicing the techniques explained in my books and workshops. In the early days these circles often began as book-study groups whose members worked — and played! — their way through one of my books chapter by chapter. Today, the leaders have usually attended in-depth workshops and trainings with me or worked with my DVD series *The Way of the Dreamer*, which demonstrates core techniques such as Lightning Dreamwork, dream reentry and tracking, and dream theater.

The basic requirement for starting an active dream group is rather simple. We need a safe, quiet space where we will not be interrupted or distracted by external noise, where it's also okay for us to make noise when we choose — for example, by drumming, singing, or acting dreams out.

As for size, the ideal size for an active dream group is probably somewhere between six and twelve people. The smaller the group, the more time that will be available for each person to share an experience and receive feedback and follow-up. The larger the group, the more dynamic the circle energy you are likely to generate. The more people with diverse viewpoints and life experiences, the more benefit you are likely to receive from multiple perspectives on a dream or incident that you share. If you want to be sure everyone in the group can explore a personal experience in depth every time you meet, then the ideal size is probably six people. However, in larger groups you will benefit from the circle energy you'll build, and — if you include group journeying and performance — you can keep everyone happily engaged throughout your session.

To get an active dream group off the ground and keep it airborne, use the following techniques.

Have a Declared Coordinator or Group Leader

In an Active Dreaming circle, everyone gets to play leader. Each member of the circle gets to lead a process — typically the Lightning Dreamwork process, described in chapter 3 — in every session. We understand that the final authority on the meaning of a dream (or a life) is the dreamer herself, and that it's our role to support her in claiming and expressing that meaning.

It's also important to have clear direction for a successful, ongoing active dream group. In my experience, this is easier to arrange when we have a single coordinator or group leader rather than a committee. It is this person's responsibility to get things done on time and keep them moving from start to stop, to maintain the protocols and ethics of our approach, and to set a dreamwork model for the group.

Commit to a Regular Schedule

Decide how often you want to meet — once a month? once a week? — and for how long (two hours is long enough if you are meeting on a weekday evening, but three hours might be right for the weekend). You may want to start with an exploratory meeting to which you'll invite new friends — for example, by announcing your group through social media and community bulletin boards. Once you have established your core group, you'll want to ask everyone to commit to attending at least six sessions.

Give Homeplay Assignments

Everyone should be asked to keep a dream journal. You'll want to set some basic reading/listening assignments. If you are going to practice Active Dreaming, everyone will work with the books, including this book, in which I explain the basic techniques.

Open with a Statement of Intention

Start each session with a short statement of intention for the group. I often open circles by having everyone join hands in a circle and then offering a statement of intention, which might include some or all of the following lines:

> We come together in a sacred and loving way
> to honor our dreams and the powers that speak through dreams,
> to find and live our essential life stories,
> and to play better games.
> We come for healing for ourselves and others.
> We come to remember who we are, where we come from, and
> what our sacred purpose is in this world and in other worlds.

Build Circle Energy

I also like to start with a simple exercise that will begin building group energy. Singing a song may accomplish this effortlessly. We might sing the Bear song I borrowed from the Mohawk, or an equally simple song that honors earth as the Mother:

> Mother, I feel you under my feet.
> Mother, I feel your heartbeat.

Make Your Space Special

Lighting a candle and placing it at the center of the circle may be sufficient to make everyone aware that you are now entering a different, and deepening, space and are willing to leave the hurry and distractions of the day behind.

Call In Dreams

Give people a moment to call up the right dream or life experience to share. In my personal circles, we drum together for a while to call in our dreams, which may be dreams of the night, incidents of the day, or fresh images that arise during the drumming. Allowing people a quiet moment to let the right dream or memory come to them may work equally well. You can also ask group members to go to the place in their bodies where they are feeling something (which might be anything at all) most strongly and let an image arise from that place.

Share Dream Titles

Go around the circle quickly and have each member share his dream title — just the title. If you have newcomers or are launching a new group, you'll want to expand this into a three-part introduction. Have each person state his name, his intention, and his dream's title.

Do Active Dreamwork

Choose the dreams you'll explore in depth. Do Lightning Dreamwork with each one. Vary the action plan each time according to the material and the group energy. If any of the dreams shared have performance potential, see if you can turn them into movement and theater and get bodies moving in the room. If a dreamer wants to reenter her dream, this is the opportunity for shared dreaming, as everyone else becomes a dream tracker traveling into her dreamscape on assignment.

Bring in Energy as Well as Information

Active dreamwork is about bringing in *energy* as well as insight. Be sure you keep things moving in the group. Do your processes within agreed-on time limits, and don't let things drag on into floppy support networking. Grab every opportunity for movement, drama, and improv.

Take It to the Community!

We need to bring the gifts of dreaming to many people who may not be ready to join a dream group but desperately need dreams in their lives. A fun assignment for your group is to ask your members to find individual ways — between sessions — to bring dreaming into the life of someone who hasn't been in the habit of sharing dreams or drawing on their guidance. This person may be an intimate family member or a complete stranger, maybe someone you meet in line at the post office or in the dentist's waiting room.

Maybe you'll find a way to create a safe space where she can tell a dream and receive some helpful feedback. Maybe you'll find yourself telling a simple story about a dream that came true, or a dream that brought healing, or how someone famous was guided by a dream — a story that might open out someone else's understanding of what dreaming might be. You'll find it vastly entertaining and inspirational to come back to your group with stories of how you brought dreams alive for others. In this way, through one encounter after another, you'll be making a beautiful contribution to the birth of our coming Commonwealth of Dreamers.

18

Community Dreaming

The stronger the imagination, the less imaginary the results.
— RABINDRANATH TAGORE

We dream for our communities and our world, as well as for ourselves and those near to us. We can learn to do this as a conscious practice in the service of peace and healing. By bringing dreams into the lives of people around us, we can heal and revitalize all our relations, our workplace, our schools, our health care, and our communities.

Harriet Tubman dreamed liberation for her people and was able to conduct three hundred escaping slaves to freedom along the Underground Railroad with the guidance of specific dreams that showed her the way to river crossings and safe houses they had never previously seen. Her story is an inspiring example of how we can dream for a whole community.

Another aspect of community dreaming is that many people may dream about the same event or issue of common concern. This happens spontaneously. It can also become a conscious practice when members of an association or organization agree to ask for dream guidance on a shared intention or develop the practice of mutual visioning.

The possibility that large numbers of people may dream about issues of community concern was recognized, and regarded as highly significant, in ancient times. In his *Oneirocritica* ("The Interpretation of Dreams," from which Freud borrowed his title), Artemidorus discussed dreams that he classified as "politic": those that occur on the same night to many of the inhabitants of a city and involve events of importance to that community.

In this chapter, we'll explore a range of Active Dreaming techniques that can be applied in the workplace, the family, and other community environments.

Dream Sharing in the Workplace

A company manager who had taken an Active Dreaming class started introducing her colleagues to the Lightning Dreamwork process. They found it so much fun — and so helpful because it gave them specific guidance — that the members of her office agreed to devote twenty minutes each morning to sharing dreams as a group. Instead of a diversion of time and energy, they found the process highly energizing and the source of creative business solutions and personal healing.

The streamlined Lightning Dreamwork process is applicable to almost any group environment. Even if only five minutes are available for group sharing, a great deal can be accomplished by having members of the group simply share the title of a dream or personal experience. These will be "thoughts for the day" and may offer specific direction. During the sharing of titles, one or more may jump out as themes that the group needs to explore that day, so you may create room to hear one or two dream reports.

Sometimes, we can change things for the better in a social or work situation simply by carrying the energy of a dream. I know a manager who was involved in bruising daily battles with a tough labor union leader. She could hardly bear to be in the same room with this man, and their personal conflict was undermining the company and labor relations. Then she dreamed that she met the labor leader in an informal setting. He was utterly charming and introduced her to his sister, who was named Charity.

She woke with completely different feelings about her workplace antagonist. Reflecting on the dream, she realized that if his sister was "Charity," his agenda might be much gentler and more compassionate than she had allowed herself to recognize. She did not tell the union guy the dream. She simply carried its energy when she went back to the negotiating table. By the end of the week, her relations with her former antagonist had been transformed; they were now on the best of terms and a difficult contract negotiation went through smoothly.

Guiding Groups to Navigate by Synchronicity

We can teach groups to do dreamwork with the incidents of waking life. In some group environments, it is initially easier to get people to discuss coincidences and chance encounters than to open up to their dream lives.

We can warm up a group to this theme very quickly by sharing a personal example of synchronicity at play and then asking other people to recount experiences of meaningful coincidence.

GROUP EXERCISE

Inviting Synchronicity

1. Write down a question or theme on which the group would like guidance. This might be a community cause ("How can we stop the toxic waste dump?" "How can we bring dreamwork into schools?").

2. Have everyone agree to make it their game to accept the first unusual or striking incident that enters their field of perception after the meeting as guidance on that theme.

3. Share your experiences, and help each other to make the link between the intention and the subsequent observation. The connection between your theme and the incident may be charming,

or it may be brutal, like the billboard that read: "You can kiss your expectations good-bye." Or there may seem to be a stretch between the theme and the incident, and imagination may be required to draw the lesson. Here's where it may be very helpful, as well as fun, to share with a group and let others release the flow of associations, just as you do when playing "If it were my dream" with dream material.

4.   Make a bumper sticker and an action plan in response to what has been learned.

People *love* to play with coincidence. Getting people in an office or community environment to talk about coincidences in their outer lives is often an easy way to get them to share more from their inner lives.

The Coincidence Card Game is great for an office or community group of any size. It quickly gets people making creative connections — as they mull over their own messages or comment on the cards others have drawn — that had previously eluded them. The ability to connect seemingly unrelated things is a characteristic of highly creative people, and the Coincidence Card Game fosters it in all the players.

Facilitating Group Dream Incubation

We can agree to dream together on a common theme. Dream incubation may not yet be a standard resource in the workplace, or even in those retreats where company employees are urged to "think outside the box," but it should be!

One corporate retreat was going nowhere until a facilitator who had attended my workshops persuaded the CEO to invite the executives to dream overnight on the main challenge facing the company. In the morning, the boss revealed that he himself had dreamed a creative solution, and the experience of dream sharing enlivened and loosened up the group, making the retreat much more rewarding than might otherwise have been the case and leading to longer-term organizational healing.

The following exercise will help you introduce the practice of dreaming on common issues to a group that may have little or no experience of dreamwork.

GROUP EXERCISE

Practicing Group Dream Incubation

1. Explain to everyone present that the group can "solve it in their sleep." Give examples of how creative ideas have come via dreams in highly practical ways. For example, how Jack Nicklaus dreamed up a new golf grip, or how Larry Page, cofounder of Google, claims the idea for the megabillion search engine first came to him in a dream, or how Stephanie Meyer got the idea for her bestselling Twilight series in a dream, preserved as chapter 13 in the first of the novels.

2. Formulate a group intention. Ask members of the group to come up with a common intention. For example: "We would like guidance on such and such." Agree that each member will write down that intention and focus on it before going to sleep.

3. Get everyone to agree to record something. Ask everyone to record whatever they remember when they wake up — even if it is a feeling, bodily sensation, or passing thought, rather than the memory of a dream experience. Emphasize that dream reports should not be edited or censored — we want the raw data!

4. Record synchronicities as well as dreams. Ask everyone also to note any unusual incidents or observations from waking life in the period before the group meets again.

5. Share with the group. Pool your dream reports and notes on synchronicity, and tell how they relate to your theme. You may notice that some of the dreams may be asking you to go beyond your original question and re-vision the whole issue.

6. Come up with a group bumper sticker and an action plan.

Growing a Community Vision

If we can come up with the right intention and a suitable gateway, we can facilitate a journey into Active Dreaming by a whole group of people in order to gain guidance and to build a shared vision for a community or organization.

Growing a community vision in this way requires an intention, a gateway image, and a method of propulsion and group focusing. A group intention is allowed to emerge from discussion. In one of my trainings, different participants offered all of the following intentions for a group journey:

> We'll grow a dream in which the first woman president of the United States is elected.

> We'll grow a vision of healing for the oceans and the fish.

> We'll dream a cure for a disease.

> We'll grow the vision of bringing dreamwork into our health-care system.

> We'll dream healing for the rage and violence that bring war and terrorism.

> We'll grow the vision of world peace.

> We'll grow the vision of a dreaming society.

I tend to prefer specific themes for group visioning, ones that enable us to focus group energy on finite goals and monitor the results.

The gateway for a journey could be an individual dream, a shared symbol, or a locale in either ordinary or nonordinary reality. I enjoy using a physical locale that is known to only one or two members of the group. If we agree to travel there, as the first stage in a group, we can often harvest impressions that can be confirmed (or otherwise) by the person who suggested the rendezvous point.

When we discover that we have seen something during the journey that we do not otherwise know about, this provides confirmation that, in a literal sense, we have gone somewhere together. For example, in one group that wanted to grow a community dream of bringing dream education into schools, a dreamer from Virginia suggested her neighborhood elementary school as a gateway point. Many of our group journeyers were able to provide accurate descriptions of details of the school that had not been supplied by the Virginia woman — the circular drive, the position of the flagpole, the locker rooms, and so on — as well as a panoply of creative ideas on manifesting the group intention.

One of the participants should be prepared to take on the role of rapporteur and cobble together a group report after the journey. This may be told as a collective dream that weaves together elements from all the journeys into a memorable story.

The process concludes, as always, with an action plan. As a summary, the following provides a model for growing a community vision.

GROUP EXERCISE

Guiding Community Visioning

1. Formulate a group intention.
2. Agree on a gateway for a group journey. This may be a locale in physical reality that is relevant to the group intention.
3. Use a drumming CD (if live drumming is not available or appropriate) to fuel and focus the group journey.
4. Choose a member of the group to act as rapporteur. He will keep notes while the other group members share journey reports.
5. Share journey reports.
6. The rapporteur weaves the individual reports and impressions into a single report — a group dream.
7. Decide on a group bumper sticker and action plan.

19

Midwives of a Dreaming Society

Say forth thy tale,
and tarry not the time.

— GEOFFREY CHAUCER

O ut in the midst of Long Island Sound, the lighthouse is winking on
its island. On a soft Sunday evening, we start my weeklong training
for teachers of Active Dreaming by creating our own beacon in the form
of clear statements of intention.

We are gathered in a circle in what used to be the living room of
Phil Donahue's beach house on the Connecticut shore. Generously, he
donated this house, SeaScape, to his neighbors, the Sisters of Mercy, who
are our hosts for the week. When I first came here, there was a mural of
two larger-than-life figures on the bow of a cruise ship. The man sported
a monocle and a dinner jacket and was hoisting a martini. The woman
was in flapper attire, with a highball. We christened them "Scott" and
"Zelda" and toasted them as our "spirit guides." Some earnest people,
since that time, must have been offended by the party people on the
wall, because the wall has been repainted flat white. Still, there is plenty
of spirit in the room tonight!

When my turn comes to speak, I announce that my intention, in opening the sixth year of my dream-teacher training, is as follows: "I am here to train and empower midwives who will help to birth a dreaming society in our time, in our world."

I look around the circle of eager, intelligent faces and know that I will not be disappointed. We have drawn wonderfully gifted and creative dreamers and healers from British Columbia and Colorado, from Rhode Island and Texas, from Minnesota and North Carolina.

I am seized by the depth of my responsibility to them, to help bring their gifts into full flower. I will make sure they have the specific tools and skills required to apply our Active Dreaming techniques to different professional and community situations and to adapt them to suit the languages and styles of different environments.

We work and play very hard over the week that unfolds. Our dream midwives regale us with marvelous stories fresh from their dreaming — of flying through the air on a purple sofa, of batting at a panther with a black patent leather pocketbook, of being entered through the spine by the luminous energy of Quetzalcoatl, the Plumed Serpent. We journey to the astral realm of the moon and back. We practice techniques of emotional and imaginal healing, and we learn how to help others to read the sign language of the world and use dreams for self-diagnosis. We practice speaking to many different kinds of audiences about why dreaming matters in our personal lives and to our kind. Our dreams and our journeys with the drum burst into dance and performance and moments of pure, unalloyed joy and laughter.

All the while, at the edge of the bushes just outside the house, three red foxes prowl. The bunny rabbits all over the property seem remarkably unfazed by foxes or humans. Only once do we see a fox with lunch in its mouth.

As the work deepens, I picture two faces, beyond those in our circle, that remind me of my responsibility — and that of the dream school — to a deeper world and a possible future. I see the face and form of a young woman who seems to live several centuries beyond our current time. I became aware of her many years ago, and I know that her life and work are connected with my own. She is a priestess and a scientist. She belongs to an order of women who are both scientists and spiritual leaders.

Their work is to rebuild our world after a series of disasters brought on by the ignorance and violence of men. Active Dreaming, as we practice it, is absolutely central to their work, and they have succeeded in creating a dreaming society among those who follow their guidance. In this possible future world, sharing dreams by a process like Lightning Dreamwork is the first business of the day. Dreaming is part of every level of education. Dream diagnosis and healing through imagery are a mainstream practice in medicine. No important policy decision is made without consultation with the dream seers — those with proven ability to scout possible futures and produce reliable information — whose independence is zealously guarded.

I hope the earth disasters that seem to have preceded the emergence of this particular dreaming society can be avoided. I also hope dream teachers of the quality of the priestess-scientist in my visions will rise to the position that she has assumed, to help heal our lives and our world.

Today, as dream guides, we can provide a safe and healing space where people from every walk of life find it possible to open their hearts and reclaim the vital energy of parts of themselves lost through trauma or heartbreak or their refusal to follow the heart's deepest desires. We can help each other to find true north, our life's flawless compass, in the thinking of the heart, so much wiser than the calculations of the head — and to gather the energy and resources required to live the path with heart, the only path worth following.

Huge numbers of people in our times are hungry for what we are offering, although few are aware, as yet, of what is offered. As dream teachers, we are called to help people find their own answers to the eternal questions — Who am I? Where do I come from? What is my life's purpose? — by reclaiming the knowledge of soul and spirit that belonged to them before they came into their present bodies.

During our week at SeaScape, I see another face that reminds me this is all about soul and recovering the energy of soul. The face is that of a small boy, maybe two years old. It is a round, freckly face under a yellow sun hat shaped like the kind we used to call a sou'wester when I was growing up in Australia. He looks very much as I did at that age. But this is not just a younger Robert. This is Dream Boy. He has a special box —

it looks like a pirate's treasure chest — that is full of dreams. If you are lucky, he will pluck the right dream from his box and send it to you.

In an especially powerful journey with the drum, I see Dream Boy flying through the air on great shining wings, and I am filled with elation. All is well when the magic that's afoot is the magic of the child who is at home in the worlds of dream and imagination and knows the power of making things up.

20

Unto the Seventh Generation

We must be mindful of the consequences of our actions down to the seventh generation after us.

— TRADITIONAL TEACHING OF THE HAUDENOSAUNEE,
OR IROQUOIS

At the Omega Institute near Rhinebeck, New York, a striking assemblage of metal figures stand on the grass beside the library. You look through the hollow in each to the last, and smallest, figure, which contains an unborn child. This installation was created by the artist Frederick Franck to honor the traditional teaching of the elders of the Six Nations of the Longhouse, or Iroquois, that we must be mindful of the consequences of our actions down to the seventh generation beyond ourselves.

One of my wishes is that, in any situation where we are called upon to choose a leader, from a president of the United States down to the coordinator of a community action group, we pose the question "Will you be mindful of the consequences of every decision down to the seventh generation beyond us?"

As I mentioned earlier, the traditional Iroquois call their chiefs *rotiyaner*, which means "men of good minds." By tradition, they are chosen by the clan mothers. When a *rotiyaner* is raised up to wear the deer antlers of office, which are set in a feathered crown, the understanding is that he will live in connection with a deeper order of purpose and responsibility. The deer antlers, rising above the physical head, symbolize the connection with a higher world, the world of spirit, where the origin and deeper logic of human events are to be found. By tradition, the "man of good mind" is accountable; if he fails to honor the trust placed in him, the women of power can and will dehorn him.

A lot of history has happened since the time of Hiawatha and the Peacemaker and the creation of the Confederacy of the Longhouse, and traditions may no longer be honored as they were meant to be, in a world turned upside down for Native Americans and others. But the tradition speaks to all peoples, I believe, and offers us a path beyond our present confusion.

In my own life, I remember my obligations to the priestess-scientist living seven generations beyond my own who has reached out to me in visions and offered me glimpses of her world, as described in the previous chapter. It is a harsh world in terms of the physical environment for human life. It is a world in which she is working with her sisterhood to restore the earth and the human spirit after a series of disasters brought about by men driven by greed and hateful ideas, men who acted with no thought for the long-term consequences of their actions.

My priestess-scientist in the seventh generation beyond mine is a dreamer in a Commonwealth of Dreamers for whom the true arts of dreaming are central to every aspect of everyday activity. Dreamers guide education and medicine; dream seers scout the best possible future for all. I am humbled by the thought that my work, in creating a new mode of Active Dreaming, may contribute to what she and her sisters are able to do. I am challenged and mobilized by the knowledge that I must give my best in the time I have available, and with the help of the community of active dreamers that is growing fast in my world, in order to help make her possible.

I came to study the ways of the Iroquois because an ancestor of the land where I now live — the Huron-Mohawk shaman I called Island Woman in *Dreamways of the Iroquois* and in my historical novel *The Firekeeper* — reached into my mind, seven generations in front of her own time, when I moved to a farm on the edge of Mohawk country in the mid-1980s. I learned from her that the vital importance of dreaming lies in its ability to help us identify what the soul (as opposed to the ego) wishes in our lives, and that dreaming is for and about communities, not only individuals.

Why do the Iroquois speak of seven generations, a phrase that has now been adopted by the sustainability movement? I don't recall ever hearing an explanation from my friends of the Six Nations or seeing one in my study of the earliest records of the traditions of the Confederacy.

But when I picture in my mind the Tree of Peace, the great white pine that stands at the center of all in the imagination of the Onkwehonwe ("the people"), the deep meaning of the number seven becomes clear in my mind and my heart.

The roots of the great tree spread out in the four cardinal directions inviting all peoples to find peace and shelter under the tree's branches. They extend east and west, north and south. They go down deep into the mystery of the Great Below. The tree rises skyward toward the Great Above, and high in its canopy perches the eagle that can see many looks away. In the heartwood of the tree, we can find our center, our true north.

As I was completing this book, I led an Active Dreaming retreat in which we stood in a circle with joined hands and sang to the seven directions. We turned first to the East, singing:

Spirit of the Wind, carry me.
Spirit of the Wind, carry me home.
Spirit of the Wind, carry me home to my soul.

Turning to the South, we sang:

Spirit of the Fire, carry me.

Turning to the West, we sang:

Spirit of the Sea, carry me.

Turning to the North, we sang:

Spirit of the Earth, carry me.

Then we faced the Great Below and sang:

Spirit of the Deep, carry me.

We turned our faces to the Great Above and sang with the sun in our eyes:

Spirit of the Sky, carry me.

Then we faced one another. The light of our heart intentions streamed toward the center of our circle. We were conscious of becoming a sphere of energy, a little world within the world. We sang:

Spirit of the heart, carry me.
Spirit of the heart, carry me home.
Spirit of the heart, carry me home to my soul.

These, for me, are the seven directions. The words of the song are not Iroquois. The first verse is borrowed from a grand old source, Anonymous. The other verses are my own. As another Native people of the Americas, the Inuit, instruct, we must come up with "fresh words" to entertain the spirits. But I think the spirit of our song is in harmony with the ancient ones of the Northeast. Certainly we sensed their benign presence. I will honor them again today with a pinch of tobacco and by giving thanks for the gifts of life, which is the way of prayer of the First Peoples. And I will remember those who are coming, seven generations beyond me, and those, seven generations back, on whose shoulders I stand. They are close to me when I listen to the wind in the trees, or relax into the flow of water, or step as an active dreamer through the veil of consensual hallucination into the Real World of the Dreamtime.

APPENDIX

Dreamland

Documents from a Possible Future

Now for something different.

I present a selection of documents received through oneiric channels that describe a future commonwealth known colloquially as Dreamland. The first appears to be an account by a sixth grader on the daily practice of dream sharing in her family. Other documents describe the practice of medicine, education, and government in a society where dreaming is central to healing and higher knowledge, and where dream seers scan possible futures and advise on all community decisions.

For the sake of balance, I include the critical report and interpolations of an investigator for the National Office of Dreams (NOD) on the content and provenance of these papers. It is not possible to date these documents with precision. Internal evidence suggests that the Dream Commonwealth was established as a "Switzerland of the mind" — and its independence and neutrality guaranteed by the world powers — in the South Pacific after an earth catastrophe known as the Singularity sometime after 2400 by our calendar. Hence, dates in the commentary are rendered as "BS" or "AS."

I

Starting the Day in Dreamland

"Who has a dream?" That's the question that starts our day at the breakfast table, or earlier when the dream won't wait.

The dream might be something that happened during the night, when you went traveling or received a visit, or got chased by monsters or chased them back. The dream might be a memory of the future. It might be something the world gave you, something you heard in the voice of a bird or the whistle of the wind in the leaves.

My dreamwork teacher says that dreaming isn't really about sleeping. It's about waking up to the things you need to know. Dreaming is traveling. You do that in your sleep, but you can do it by stepping inside the world of a tree, or walking the path of moonlight on water, or, as my little sister says, by just punching a hole in the world. When we go dreaming, we step through the curtain of the world into the world-behind-the-world. Out there are beings who are dreaming about us. Sometimes they come poking or tickling through the curtain of our world to help us wake up. This is called coincidence, and if you want to get good at dreaming, you watch it the way a cat watches a bird.

In our house, when there's toast and jam on the table, we take turns telling dreams and coincidences. Whoever has the strongest feelings gets to go first.

Every game requires rules, and we have rules for dream telling. The first rule is about time. When we start a dream telling, we set the egg timer (ours looks like a bear) for ten minutes. You get five minutes to tell your dream, and then everyone gets five minutes more to talk it over with you and help you figure out what to do. Then the egg timer goes off and everything stops, or else the bear gets really, really mad. We go on to the next story, or we head off to work and school.

We set the timer even on lazy days when we could take hours and hours to hang out with a dream. We might do lots of things with a dream after a telling, like making a picture, or logging on the metalibrary to check out a funny word, or letting a neighbor know how to avoid an accident next Tuesday, or traveling back inside the dreamspace to play with a friend or deal with an enemy or get the words of a song. But we want to do the first sharing fast because it's fun, and because that way you don't lose the energy. "Like lightning!" my dreamwork teacher says, sawing his hand down like a lightning bolt. "Do it fast and feel the power!"

A big rule is that we must tell our dream as a story, and everyone present must listen up. It's okay to act the dream out as you tell it, slithering around the floor or turning pirouettes of fire. You want to give your dream a name; stories need titles.

When you've told your dream, the other people get to ask you a few — just a few — questions. The first question is always "What did you feel when you woke up?" What you feel in your heart or your tummy about a dream is the best guide to whether the dream is good or bad and whether it's about something in this world, or another world, or it's one of the messages coded in symbols that bring the worlds together.

Another question we always ask is "Could anything in the dream happen in the future in some way?" We search every dream for clues to the future, because in dreams we are time travelers who can scout out the roads ahead for ourselves and others. When a dream opens a door on the future, we want to figure out whether the event on the other side is fixed or squidgy. A squidgy future is one we can push or pull like Play-Doh, so things will come out better.

After the questions, everyone who is playing the Lightning Dreamwork game gets to say anything they like about the dream as long as they say it politely. To do this, we begin by saying, "If this were my dream," and then add whatever pops into our heads.

We're watching the egg timer, because we're not done until we get to the Action Plan. Dreams require action.

Lucy (she's my sister, and she's four) is jumping up and down now, so I have to let her speak. I hope she'll be quick.

Lucy: I want to tell them what we do with S-C-A-R-Y dreams.
Me: Okay.
Lucy: You spit out the bad stuff right away on the ground or down the toilet. If there's something in your dream that was chasing you, you go back inside and you chase it back.
Me: But what if it's too scary?
Lucy (holding up a teddy bear as big as she is): Then you take a special friend with you — we call it an ally — who can scare it back. When you brave up to what was scaring you, sometimes it becomes a new friend.

Me: Anything else you want to tell us about scary dreams?

Lucy: They show you bad stuff that can't be stopped unless you tell Mommy or Daddy and they make it right. Like when I dreamed the crash.

Me: Right.

Lucy: And I told Mommy, and we didn't go on the red shuttle that went boom.

Me: Thank you, Lucy.

Lucy: No, wait. Tell them if you're falling you should stop flapping and start flying.

That was Lucy. She's taken up all the time I had left. I have to prepare for my prevision final at school. I dreamed the questions last night, of course, but I have to go over my notes.

Then we are having a special visitor, a professor from the scholar city of Anamnesis. He's going to give us a special assignment. Using sonic driving, we get to journey to a different time and enter the mind of someone in that time. We then have to write an auto-biography as that person and also prepare a research report on new data we have collected using the metalibrary. Everyone's excited by this. The student who gets the top score will be invited to be a summer intern at the School of Dream Archaeology, and they have really cool stuff there.

ANALYST'S NOTE: Though a child ("Lucy") is given a first name, the identity of the narrator — apparently a school-age child with a mature vocabulary — does not appear in the document supra, as transmitted to this office. The following documents are in a different, adult voice; for a tentative attribution, see my report infra.

II

Doctors in Dreamland

Our doctors are dreamers. No one in Dreamland would consider diagnosing or prescribing without consulting dreams. In our medical schools, we learn, as Galen already knew, that the dreaming mind can travel throughout the body and report on its condition in exact detail. A change in a single cell can be detected in a dream many years before the condition has spread far enough to produce detectable physical symptoms.

Many of our physicians have signs on their walls that read: MY PATIENT IS MY COLLEAGUE. Some have expanded this into a personal charter. One of the ways doctors and patients learn from each other is by swapping dreams.

But dream diagnosis begins long before a visit to a doctor's office, in regular dream sharing and — where the dreamer feels that a specialist's knowledge may be required — in wellness or preneed clinics, where the dream helpers are often nurses.

Imagery harvesting is central in the treatment of illness. Our approach is that *any* dream image can offer a path to healing if it is worked correctly. This often requires continuing the dream, frequently with the aid of a helper who accompanies the dreamer on a conscious journey back into the dreamscape. The following is an example from one of our classic manuals of imaginal healing.

Meeting Spider Woman

An artist is terrified by a recurring dream of a jumping spider that grows bigger and bigger until it takes over her studio. With the help of a dream guide, she agrees to reenter the dream in a conscious journey, with the focused intention of facing her terror and finding out what is to be done. The guide, seated beside her and holding her hand, will support her throughout the journey.

Back inside her dream, the artist has no trouble finding the spider. She is terrified again as it grows until it is larger than human size, but she stands her ground. Now the spider shapeshifts into Spider Woman and tells her, "Because you found the courage to meet me, I will give you the power to reweave the energy web of your body and the web of possibility in your life."

The dreamer was facing a biopsy. The results

showed she was cancer-free. She embarked on the most creative period of her personal and artistic life.

As in this example, dream reentry is one of our core techniques for healing. A personal image provides the doorway for a conscious journey in which the dreamer may be accompanied by a friend or guide or even a whole family of dream travelers. Relaxation and focused intention are the keys to this mode of conscious dream travel. In many cases, sonic driving (especially when generated by live shamanic drumming) is used to deepen and accelerate the journey.

Some dreams provide portals for soul recovery, an essential mode of healing that the ancestor shamans helped us to reclaim, to save at least some of our kind from joining the march of the husk people, the living dead. Shamans know that soul loss — the loss of vital energy and identity — is at the root of illness and despair. We lose vital soul through grief and trauma and heartbreak, through wrenching life choices that leave us divided against ourselves, through habits of deceit and addiction that drive our bright spirits to abandon us in disgust. Soul loss can reduce us to the condition of the walking dead, passionless and dreary, forever trying to fit in with other people's needs and expectations, lost to any sense of purpose.

Dreams show us where our missing parts may have gone and invite us to reach in and bring them back. When we dream again and again of the "old place" (maybe a childhood home, maybe a space we shared with a former partner), we may be learning that a part of us is stuck in that place or went missing at the time we lived there. By going back inside the dream of the old place, we may be able to locate that lost aspect of our own identity and energy and find the way to bring it back into our heart and life.

In the hearthstone circles where we gather with our intentional families at least one evening a week, we tend the dreams that show us where the soul has gone, and we help each other, with fierce compassion, to bring it home.

Our flying doctors work with the souls of the dead, as

well as with the souls of the living. Our best clues to where we are needed come from spontaneous night dreams in which sleepers receive visitations from the departed and travel, often unconsciously, into realms where the departed are at home. Such encounters can be the source of much-needed healing, forgiveness, and closure, as well as mutual guidance. When they are released from the second body, the departed may become wise counselors and "family angels." Prior to that liberation, they may need help from our healers because they are enmeshed in the sticky stuff of old cravings, rancor, and desire. "The living have the ability to assist the imaginations of the dead," as the poet said. Our flying doctors operate in this understanding, on both sides of the swing-door of physical death.

The First Peoples of the land where we built our dreaming city say that the big stories — the stories that want to be told and to be lived — are hunting their tellers, like predators in the bush or sharks in the water. In healing, as in education and family life, we are constantly engaged in helping each other to let the big story come through.

III

Remember Montezuma

In the capstone of the dolmen arch that leads to the Grove of the Seers, a phrase has been chiseled: "Remember Montezuma."

Every fourth grader knows what this means. It is one of the lessons the world forgot before the Singularity, an object lesson in what happens to a society that ceases to listen to its dreamers. Before the Aztecs ever laid eyes on a European, people in Mexico were dreaming strange and terrible things. They saw temples being burned and cities destroyed.

The emperor Montezuma ordered the most respected dreamers to be brought before him. Eyes cast to the floor, they told him of things they lacked words to describe, of fearsome mountains moving on the waves, of metal serpents spewing fire. The emperor rewarded the dreamers by having them thrown into prison and starved to death exquisitely slowly. After that, nobody wanted to tell Montezuma their dreams.

Montezuma succeeded in blinding his empire. When the mountains moving on the waters turned out to be the ships of the conquistadors, the Aztecs were completely unprepared. "Those who die are those who do not understand; those who live will understand it," the Mayans wrote in their book of prophecies, the Chilam Balam.

Because it is so remote, this story is less painful than that of the dreamers of our own families who were ignored before the Singularity. The message flashes from the distant mirror. If we can see the future, we may be able to change it for the better.

Our dream seers are identified young, sometimes before they have started school. The first sign of the gift is usually simple: the child dreams an event that subsequently takes place. Or the child hears the voices of the speaking land and receives messages from birds and animals.

We understand that all of us are dreaming the future, all the time, and that we not only have previsions of coming events but are also able to scout out alternative possible futures. All dreams are scanned for clues to the future. This is the most important function of the Stream. Every resident of our commonwealth is requested to enter a brief dream report in a home terminal every day, contributing to the Stream, from which common themes and details are extracted by data spiders before they are reviewed by trained readers employed by the Grove.

From the earliest possible age, we confirm for our children that dreaming the future is entirely natural. We also help them to understand that any future we can see, in dreams or in the workings of our seers, is a possible future, and that it is often possible to change the odds on the manifestation of a specific future event. When it appears impossible for an individual to change certain future events perceived in dreams — such as natural disasters or death at an advanced age — the dream information can still be employed in a useful way. For example, we can alert friends not to go on vacation in the place where the dreamed hurricane will hit, or we can help someone whose death is near, and help that person's family to meet that situation with grace and closure.

Our dream seers travel not only to the past and future but also between alternate timelines. We are constantly experimenting with the possibility that in this way we can help choose an event track — maybe one of infinite alternative possible event tracks — that will be followed in the world. In the language of BS physics, this could be represented as a case of the observer effect operating on a human scale. At quantum levels, the act of observation plucks a specific phenomenon out of a cauldron of possibilities. We operate differently in our practice of dreaming: through the act of observation, we select a certain event track that will begin to be manifested in the physical world. By a fresh act of observation, or re-visioning, we can then proceed to alter that event track or switch to an entirely different one.

Access to the seers of Dreamland is immensely prized. We receive delegations from all the world powers, who come to us in the same way that the ancient envoys sailed to the oracle at Delphi to consult the source that "neither reveals nor conceals the truth, but signifies." Visiting deputations are closely observed by our Watchers. Outside powers are constantly seeking to undermine our neutrality, corrupt our seership, and steal our gifts. They have even attempted to kidnap some of our gifted children. We intend to substitute holo-conferencing for physical visits to Dreamland, and to insist that official traffic be routed through a single agency, the National Office of Dreams (NOD), in each government with which we have a service contract.

IV

A Switzerland of the Mind

Dreamland is not in the world of BS.

Unfortunately, it probably could not have come into being without the Singularity that nearly ended the long experiment with human consciousness on the planet. The devastating events associated with the Singularity do not need to be recalled here. The prophet of the Longhouse People called this "the Day Great Turtle Rose to Shake Humans off Her Back." The memory is scored deep in the collective psyche and will never be erased, though in the world outside Dreamland, Big Pharma is up to its old games, mass-producing drugs that suppress memory and dreaming on the pretext of correcting TTSD (transtemporal stress disorder). Such medications are banned in Dreamland, along with hallucinogens and oneiric enhancement drugs.

The precise location of Dreamland will not be given here, to discourage speculation in real estate. [ANALYST'S NOTE: This sentence is obviously BS; see report below.] *But it is not necessary to conceal the special link between Dreamland and the Commonwealth of Oz, renowned for its native Dreamers. The Ozzies were better prepared for the Singularity than other national entities because of their remarkable and prescient investment in huge desalinization programs, so that what remains of a continent that was once mostly desert is now green.*

Dreamland is not the official name of the Commonwealth of Dreamers, though they are happy for others to use it. The major world powers are all bound by treaty to defend its status as a protected territory that must remain neutral in all international disputes: a Switzerland of the mind.

Dreamland has no military forces. However, it has a corps of Watchers that includes a Fighter Wing, trained in advanced methods of psychic combat, that must always be commanded by a woman.

In place of a constitution, Dreamland has a charter that the founders titled "Rules for Herding Cats." One of the rules reads as follows:

"When a decision is required on a matter of community importance, the people must come together in the Big House and make a web."

In the first years of Dreamland, when the community was small, there was only one Big House, built of very simple materials around a great tree that rose through the roof like a ladder to the sky. Now Dreamland has many Big Houses, but the making of a dreaming web is essentially the same. Standing in a great circle at nightfall as they sing songs of the earth, the weavers raise the Mother's energy into the vital centers and share it hand to hand, giving and receiving. When the energy is flowing strong between them, they each project ropelike energy cords to a common center and begin to weave and shape the web. The cords flash with many colors, but as they interweave they glow sparkling white. When the chief weavers are satisfied that the web is strong enough to serve the group intention, the dreamers lie down in a cartwheel configuration on the floor.

Lying together in the dark, with their web of dreaming glowing above and around them, the dreamers sing their group intention over and over. As they sing, the web grows. It grows until it has brought within it everything the dreamers need to see and know. As the energy filaments stretch, they may encompass the whole planet. All points in time are accessible. Years or centuries may slip by, like blown leaves, in the group perception. While the group visions together within the web, the individual Dreamers move along its strands, agile as human spiders, and drop down on scenes they choose to see close up.

At daybreak, the Dreamers share their perceptions, and the necessary decision becomes clear. They say there is no need to count heads when hearts are joined and connected to the heart of the Mother.

The Meaning of Anamnesis

The great scholar city of Dreamland is called Anamnesis. The name evokes the Platonic doctrine that all true wisdom consists in overcoming the amnesia that comes with the journey through the birth canal and that is deepened by the miasmic conditions of human society. As a practice, anamnesis is soul remembering: reclaiming the knowledge that belonged to the soul before it descended into the body and acting on that knowledge.

To this end, the sages of Anamnesis have constructed a House of

Time, which offers many portals for conscious dream journeys on which to explore the nature of the multidimensional self and engage in direct communication with teachers above the fourth level of the astral plane. [ANALYST'S NOTE: Here the text file becomes corrupt; it may have been deliberately scrambled.]

From the Report by Tsu-lin Wu, Investigator for the National Office of Dreams (NOD), New Beijing, October 1, 330 AS

This office respectfully offers a preliminary assessment of materials recently acquired for the ongoing longitudinal study of the oneiric entity. It is noted that the provenance of these documents remains obscure. The author of the first and somewhat colloquial paper ("Starting the Day in Dreamland") appears to be a sixth-grade student who recorded and incorporated the experiences of younger siblings. Her mature tone and the settled family circumstances suggest that she was writing at least thirty years AS (After Singularity), and I believe this document to be authentic.

The remaining documents are problematic. They are rife with anachronisms and inconsistencies, and references (which I have checked and corrected, as necessary) are all to BS (Before Singularity) sources. Documents II, III, and IV may be derived from a work of utopian fiction titled *A Switzerland of the Mind*, published three years before the Singularity. This is the famous "lost book" of the Dreamers. No authenticated copy survives, unless in the library of Anamnesis, which is closed to us. Yet the Dreamers regard the author as one of the founders of their oneiric polity. No critical reader could fail to notice the fictional element in Document II ("Doctors in Dreamland"); who would ever believe that every doctor, in any kind of society, could agree to the pledge "My patient is my colleague"?

At my last holo-conference with the Dreamers, I requested their feedback on these documents. The request was ignored. They spent the whole period of the interview impugning our Big Pharma. The one who projected a whole-body avatar with gills and the head of a salmon bubbled defamation against our president and dared to allege that our enlightened government, in concert with Big Pharma, is involved in a conspiracy to "cage the minds of the people" through unlimited virtual sex and drugs that suppress the dreaming function, while releasing a "psychotic elite" supercharged by "oneiric Viagra and dream steroids." I have forwarded the holo-record of this disturbing interview to the appropriate authorities.

I recommend that permission for publication of the foregoing documents in any form be denied.

I also respectfully request that I be relieved from my present liaison duties with the Dreamers. Since I listened to their Salmon Speaker, my nights are filled with a chaos of water, and when I seek a second opinion from the Book of Changes, it is always the same: K'an. The deluge. Falling into the abyss. For three years one does not find the way. Yet (the senior diviner reminds me) the commentary adds that water is always true to itself. Is this how we dreamed BS?

ACKNOWLEDGMENTS

My students are my teachers. I am deeply indebted to the many adventurers in consciousness who have come to my workshops and Active Dreaming circles in North America, Europe, and Australia. The journeys we have made together have helped me to develop and refine the techniques explained in this book and have produced many of its best stories.

I want to acknowledge the many fine scholars and dream researchers who have generously shared the fruits of their investigations into the history, anthropology, and psychology of dreaming, including Rita Dwyer, Stanley Krippner, Patricia Garfield, Deidre Barrett, Aad van Ouwerkerk, Jean Campbell, Kelly Bulkeley, Iain Edgar, Barbara Tedlock, Jeremy Taylor, Charles Stewart, Bob Hoss, Robert Gongloff, Robert Waggoner, Wewer and Steve Keohane, Henry Reed, Joanne Rochon, Carlos Smith, Alan Worsley, and the late Claire Sylvia. Michael Harner, Sandra Ingerman, and Timothy White helped me to explore the core techniques of shamanism I melded with dreamwork to produce the approach I call Active Dreaming.

I salute the adventurers in consciousness who have joined me since 1996 in very special retreats on a mountain in the New York Adirondacks and in other advanced programs where we have test-flown new Active Dreaming techniques and embarked on group journeys into the multiverse. I am grateful to the wonderful volunteer coordinators who have helped to bring my workshops into many communities; they include Jane E. Carleton, Donna Katsuranis, Karen Silverstein, Irene D'Alessio, Carol Davis, Rita Baniene, Irene Boulu, Stephanie Deignan, Jenny Noble, Karen McKean, Nancy Friedman, Steffani LaZier, Suzette Rios-Scheurer, Elizabeth Dimarco and Jeni Hogenson

Thanks, also, to the wonderful people who have provided dream settings for group adventures in Active Dreaming: at the Omega Institute, at Esalen, at Kripalu, at Naropa University, at the New York Open Center, at John F. Kennedy University, at Mercy-by-the-Sea, at the Hameau de l'Etoile, at Garnet Hill Lodge, at Mosswood Hollow, and at many other places.

Georgia Hughes, editorial director at New World Library, is a dream editor and her colleagues are a dream team. I celebrate all of them, including visionary publisher Marc Allen, master wave-catcher Munro Magruder, dream editors Kristen Cashman and Jonathan Wichmann, tireless publicists Monique Muhlenkamp and Kim Corbin, Danielle Galat, Ami Parkerson, Tona Pearce Myers, and Tracy Cunningham, with her fabulous designing eye.

Bear hugs for the "frequent fliers" who have joined me in all the adventures in group dream travel, shamanic theater, and imaginal healing, from Copenhagen to Cincinnati, from Sydney to San Francisco. I have no biological siblings, but I adopt some from time to time, and two of my dream sisters, Wanda Burch and Carol Davis, have been peerless companions on the roads of this world and the world-behind-the-world for more than two decades. Lion purrs for my wife, Marcia, my best friend and counselor in all seasons, and for my daughters, who, when very young and very close to the dreaming, demonstrated again and again how the imagination can create worlds.

NOTES

1. Carl G. Jung, "Approaching the Unconscious," in *Man and His Symbols* (New York: Doubleday, 1964), p. 102.
2. Natalie Angier, "Modern Life Suppresses Ancient Body Rhythm," *New York Times*, March 14, 1995.
3. A. Roger Ekirch, "Sleep We Have Lost: Pre-industrial Slumber in the British Isles," *American Historical Review* 106, no. 2 (April 2001): 243–386.
4. Kate Murphy, "Take a Look Inside My Dream," *New York Times*, July 9, 2010.
5. C. G. Jung, *Children's Dreams: Notes from the Seminar Given in 1936–1940*, ed. Lorenz Jung and Maria Meyer-Grass, trans. Ernst Falzeder (Princeton, NJ: Princeton University Press, 2008), p. 332.
6. Henry Reed, *Dream Medicine* (Mouth of Wilson, VA: Hermes Home, 2005), p. 13.
7. Mircea Eliade, *Journal III, 1970–1978*, trans. Teresa Lavender Fagan (Chicago: University of Chicago Press, 1989), p. 165.
8. Synesius of Cyrene, "On Dreams," in *The Essays and Hymns of Synesius of Cyrene*, trans. Augustine Fitzgerald (Oxford: Oxford University Press, 1930), pp. 328–329.

9. Frederik van Eeden, a Dutch psychologist and novelist, is credited with coining the term *lucid dream* in his paper "A Study of Dreams," published in *Proceedings of the Society for Psychical Research*, vol. 26 (Glasgow: Robert Maclehose and Company, 1913).

10. C. G. Jung, *Psychological Types* (1921), in *Collected Works*, vol. 6, trans. Gerhard Adler (Princeton, NJ: Bollingen, 1976), para. 644.

11. C. S. Lewis, "On Three Ways of Writing for Children" (1952), in *Of Other Worlds* (New York: Harcourt, Brace, 1967), p. 25.

12. Dorothea Hover-Kramer, *Second Chance at Your Dream* (Santa Rosa, CA: Energy Psychology Press, 2009), p. 47.

13. Jelaluddin Rumi, "The Guest House," in *The Essential Rumi*, trans. Coleman Barks, with John Moyne (Edison, NJ: Castle Books, 1997), p. 109.

14. Kathleen Norris, *Acedia & Me* (New York: Riverhead Books, 2008), p. 3.

15. Lewis Richmond, "Fear of Public Speaking," March 2, 2010, Aging as a Spiritual Practice, http://agingasaspiritualpractice.com/2010/03/02/fear -of-public-speaking/.

16. Giovanni Pico della Mirandola, "Oration on the Dignity of Man," n.d., Center for the Study of Complex Systems, http://cscs.umich .edu/~crshalizi/Mirandola/.

17. Carolyn Myss, *Anatomy of the Spirit: The Seven Stages of Power and Healing* (New York: Three Rivers, 1996).

18. Marie-Louise von Franz, "The Process of Individuation," in *Man and His Symbols*, ed. Carl G. Jung (New York: Dell, 1968), p. 235, and in *Individuation in Fairy Tales* (Boston: Shambhala, 2001).

19. The fantasy writer and editor Terri Windling discusses Madame d'Aulnoy's story in a marvelous book on fairy tales and survivors titled *The Armless Maiden* and in an essay, "Les contes des fées: The Literary Fairy Tales of France," (2000), which is available online at the Endicott Studio, www.endicott-studio.com/rdrm/forconte.html.

20. Michael Meade, *The World Behind the World* (Seattle: GreenFire, 2008), p. 2.

21. Ruth Sawyer, *The Way of the Storyteller* (New York: Penguin, 1977), pp. 20, 28.

22. Viktor Frankl, *Man's Search for Meaning* (New York: Pocket Books, 1985), p. 95.

23. Ibid., p. 131.

24. Martha Beckwith, *Hawaiian Mythology* (1940; reprint, Honolulu: University of Hawai'i Press, 1976), pp. 130, 492.

25. Charles Montgomery, *The Shark God: Encounters with Ghosts and Ancestors in the South Pacific* (New York: HarperCollins, 2004), p. 269.

26. C. G. Jung, *The Red Book: Liber Novus*, ed. Sonu Shamdasani (New York: Norton, 2009), p. 273.

27. C. G. Jung, "On Synchronicity," lecture delivered at the 1951 Eranos conference, published in *The Structure and Dynamics of the Psyche*, in *Collected Works*, vol. 8, trans. R. F. C. Hull (Princeton, NJ: Bollingen, 1976), para. 970. See also Jung, "Synchronicity: An Acausal Connecting Principle," in ibid., paras. 826–827.

28. Marie-Louise von Franz, *Projection and Re-collection in Jungian Psychology*, trans. William H. Kennedy (LaSalle, IL: Open Court, 1990), p. 190; italics in the original.

29. C. G. Jung, *Mysterium Coniunctionis: An Inquiry into the Separation and Synthesis of Psychic Opposites in Alchemy*, in *Collected Works*, vol. 14, trans. R. F. C. Hull (Princeton, NJ: Bollingen, 1976), para. 765.

30. Anne Lombard-Jourdan, *Aux origines du carnaval* (Paris: Odile Jacob, 2005), pp. 139–141.

31. Jung, "On Synchronicity," para. 816.

32. J. P. Eckermann, *Conversations with Goethe*, quoted in Jung, "On Synchronicity," para. 860.

33. Rina Swentzell and Sandra P. Edelman, "The Butterfly Effect," *El Palacio* 95, no. 1 (Fall–Winter 1989).

34. David Whyte, *Crossing the Unknown Sea: Work as a Pilgrimage of Identity* (New York: Riverhead Books, 2001), p. 121.

35. Jean Houston, *Jump Time* (New York: Jeremy P. Tarcher/Putnam, 2000).

36. Lyanda Lynn Haupt, *Crow Planet: Essential Wisdom from the Urban Wilderness* (New York: Little, Brown, 2010).

37. Ibid., p. 7.

38. Ralph Waldo Emerson, "Spiritual Laws," in *The Essential Writings of Ralph Waldo Emerson*, ed. Brooks Atkinson (New York: Modern Library, 2000), p. 177.

39. Peter Block, *Community: The Structure of Belonging* (San Francisco: Berrett-Koehler, 2009), p. 21.

SELECTED BIBLIOGRAPHY

Ackerman, Diane. *Deep Play*. New York: Vintage, 1999.

Baldwin, Christina. *Storycatcher*. Novato, CA: New World Library, 2005.

Beaudet, Denyse. *Dreamguider: Open the Door to Your Child's Dreams*. Charlottesville, VA: Hampton Roads, 2008.

Becker, Raymond de. *The Understanding of Dreams and Their Influence on the History of Man*. New York: Bell, 1968.

Beckwith, Martha. *Hawaiian Mythology*. 1940. Reprint, Honolulu: University of Hawai'i Press, 1976.

Berndt, Ronald M., and Catherine H. Berndt. *The Speaking Land: Myth and Story in Aboriginal Australia*. Rochester, VT: Inner Traditions, 1994.

Block, Peter. *The Answer to How Is Yes*. San Francisco: Berrett-Koehler, 2003.

———. *Community: The Structure of Belonging*. San Francisco: Berrett-Koehler, 2009.

Borges, Jorge Luis. *Labyrinths*. New York: New Directions, 1964.

Borges, Jorge Luis, with Silvina Ocampo and A. Bioy Casares, eds. *The Book of Fantasy*. New York: Viking, 1988.

Boyd, Brian. *On the Origin of Stories: Evolution, Cognition and Fiction*. Cambridge, MA: Harvard University Press, Belknap Press, 2009.

Burch, Wanda Easter. *She Who Dreams: A Journey into Healing through Dreamwork.* Novato, CA: New World Library, 2003.

Caillois, Roger, ed. *The Dream Adventure.* New York: Orion, 1963.

Campbell, Jean. *Dreams beyond Dreaming.* Virginia Beach: Donning, 1980.

Campbell, Joseph. *The Hero with a Thousand Faces.* Novato, CA: New World Library, 2008.

———. *The Way of the Animal Powers.* San Francisco: Alfred van der Marck/ Harper & Row, 1983.

Carse, James P. *Finite and Infinite Games.* New York: Random House, 1986.

Cooper, Andrew. *Playing in the Zone: Exploring the Spiritual Dimensions of Sports.* Boston: Shambhala, 1998.

Corbin, Henry. *Creative Imagination in the Sufism of Ibn 'Arabi.* Translated by Ralph Mannheim. Princeton, NJ: Bollingen, 1981.

———. *The Man of Light in Iranian Sufism.* Translated by Nancy Pearson. New Lebanon, NY: Omega, 1994.

Csikszentmihalyi, Mihaly. *Creativity: Flow and the Psychology of Discovery and Invention.* New York: HarperCollins, 1996.

———. *Flow: The Psychology of Optimal Experience.* New York: Harper & Row, 1990.

Dante Alighieri. *Purgatorio.* Verse translation by W. S. Merwin. New York: Knopf, 2000.

Davies, Robertson. *The Deptford Trilogy.* New York: Penguin, 1990.

de la Mare, Walter, ed. *Behold, the Dreamer!* New York: Knopf, 1939.

Dossey, Larry. *Healing Words.* San Francisco: HarperSanFrancisco, 1993.

Ekirch, A. Roger. *At Day's Close: Night in Times Past.* New York: Norton, 2005.

Eliot, T. S. *Four Quartets.* 1945. Reprint, San Diego: Harvest/Harcourt, n.d.

Emerson, Ralph Waldo. *The Essential Writings of Ralph Waldo Emerson.* Edited by Brooks Atkinson. New York: Modern Library, 2000.

Frankl, Viktor. *Man's Search for Meaning.* New York: Pocket Books, 1985.

Freud, Sigmund. *The Psychopathology of Everyday Life.* Translated by A. A. Brill. London: E. Benn, 1935.

Garfield, Patricia. *Creative Dreaming.* New York: Ballantine, 1976.

Gladwell, Malcolm. *Outliers.* New York: Little, Brown, 2008.

Harjo, Joy. *How We Became Human: New and Selected Poems.* New York: Norton, 2004.

Haupt, Lyanda Lynn. *Crow Planet: Essential Wisdom from the Urban Wilderness.* New York: Little, Brown, 2009.

Houston, Jean. *Jump Time.* New York: Jeremy P. Tarcher/Putnam, 2000.

Hover-Kramer, Dorothea. *Second Chance at Your Dream*. Santa Rosa, CA:
Energy Psychology Press, 2009.

Huizinga, Johan. *Homo Ludens: A Study of the Play Element in Culture*. Boston:
Beacon, 1955.

Humphrey, Caroline, with Urgunge Onon. *Shamans and Elders: Experience,
Knowledge and Power among the Daur Mongols*. Oxford: Clarendon, 1996.

Jung, C. G. *Children's Dreams: Notes from the Seminar Given in 1936–1940*.
Edited by Lorenz Jung and Maria Meyer-Grass. Translated by Ernst
Falzeder. Princeton, NJ: Princeton University Press, 2008.

———. *Man and His Symbols*. New York: Dell, 1968.

———. *Memories, Dreams, Reflections*. Edited by Aniela Jaffé. New York:
Vintage, 1965.

———. *Psychology and Religion: West and East*. Translated by R. F. C. Hull.
Princeton, NJ: Princeton University Press, 1969.

———. *The Red Book: Liber Novus*. Edited by Sonu Shamdasani. New York:
Norton, 2009.

———. *Synchronicity: An Acausal Connecting Principle*. Translated by R. F. C.
Hull. Princeton, NJ: Princeton University Press/Bollinger, 1973.

Kimmins, C. W. *Children's Dreams*. London: Longman's, Green, 1920.

Krippner, Stanley, and David Feinstein. *Personal Mythology*. New York: Jeremy P.
Tarcher/Perigee, 1988.

Larsen, Stephen. *The Mythic Imagination*. Rochester, VT: Inner Traditions, 1996.

Lombard-Jourdan, Anne. *Aux origines du carnaval*. Paris: Odile Jacob, 2005.

Long, Max Freedom. *The Secret Science behind Miracles*. Marina del Rey, CA:
DeVorss, 1976.

McKnight, John, and Peter Block. *The Abundant Community*. San Francisco:
Berrett-Koehler, 2010.

Meade, Michael. *The World Behind the World*. Seattle: GreenFire, 2008.

Meier, C. A., ed. *Atom and Archetype: The Pauli/Jung Letters, 1932–1958*.
Translated by David Roscoe. Princeton, NJ: Princeton University Press,
2001.

Miller, Arthur I. *Insights of Genius: Imagery and Creativity in Science and Art*.
New York: Copernicus/Springer-Verlag, 1996.

Montgomery, Charles. *The Shark God: Encounters with Ghosts and Ancestors in
the South Pacific*. New York: HarperCollins, 2004.

Moss, Robert. *Conscious Dreaming*. New York: Three Rivers, 1996.

———. *The Dreamer's Book of the Dead*. Rochester, VT: Destiny Books, 2005.

———. *Dreamgates: Exploring the Worlds of Soul, Imagination, and Life beyond
Death*. Novato, CA: New World Library, 2010.

————. *Dreaming True.* New York: Pocket Books, 2000.

————. *Dreamways of the Iroquois.* Rochester, VT: Destiny Books, 2005.

————. *The Secret History of Dreaming.* Novato, CA: New World Library, 2009.

————. *The Three "Only" Things: Tapping the Power of Dreams, Coincidence, and Imagination.* Novato, CA: New World Library, 2007.

Myss, Carolyn. *Anatomy of the Spirit: The Seven Stages of Power and Healing.* New York: Three Rivers, 1996.

Nachmanovitch, Stephen. *Free Play: Improvisation in Life and Art.* New York: Jeremy P. Tarcher/Putnam, 1990.

Norris, Kathleen. *Acedia & Me.* New York: Riverhead Books, 2008.

Oliver, Mary. *New and Selected Poems.* Boston: Beacon, 1992.

Pearson, Carol. *The Hero Within.* San Francisco: Harper & Row, 1986.

Plato. *Collected Dialogues.* Edited by Edith Hamilton and Huntington Cairnes. Princeton, NJ: Bollingen, 1989.

Plutarch. "Concerning the Face Which Appears in the Orb of the Moon." In *Moralia,* vol. 12. Translated by Harold Cherniss and William Helmbold. Cambridge, MA: Harvard University Press, 1995.

————. "The Obsolescence of Oracles." In *Moralia,* vol. 12. Translated by Harold Cherniss and William Helmbold. Cambridge, MA: Harvard University Press, 1995.

————. "On the Delays of the Divine Vengeance." In *Moralia,* vol. 7. Translated by Philip H. DeLacy and Benedict Einarson. Cambridge, MA: Harvard University Press, 1959.

Poirier, Sylvie. "This Is Good Country. We Are Good Dreamers: Dreams and Dreaming in the Australian Western Desert." In *Dream Travelers: Sleep Experiences and Culture in the Western Pacific,* edited by Roger Ivar Lohmann, pp. 107–126. New York: Palgrave Macmillan, 2003.

Powers, Ron. *Mark Twain: A Life.* New York: Free Press, 2005.

Reed, Henry. *Dream Medicine.* Mouth of Wilson, VA: Hermes Home, 2005.

————. *Edgar Cayce on Channeling Your Higher Self.* New York: Warner, 1989.

Roberts, Jane. *The Nature of Personal Reality.* New York: Bantam, 1990.

Rumi, Jelaluddin. *The Essential Rumi.* Translated by Coleman Barks, with John Moyne. Edison, NJ: Castle Books, 1997.

Sardello, Robert. *Facing the World with Soul.* New York: HarperCollins, 1994.

Sawyer, Ruth. *The Way of the Storyteller.* New York: Penguin, 1977.

Shulman, David, and Guy G. Stroumsa, eds. *Dream Cultures: Explorations in the Comparative History of Dreaming.* New York: Oxford University Press, 1999.

Spangler, David. *Blessing.* New York: Riverhead Books, 2002.

Sumegi, Angela. *Dreamworlds of Shamanism and Tibetan Buddhism: The Third Place*. Albany: State University of New York Press, 2008.

Synesius of Cyrene. *The Essays and Hymns of Synesius of Cyrene*. Translated by Augustine Fitzgerald. 2 vols. Oxford: Oxford University Press, 1930.

Talbot, Michael. *The Holographic Universe*. New York: Harper Perennial, 1992.

Tedlock, Barbara, ed. *Dreaming: Anthropological and Psychological Interpretations*. Santa Fe: School of American Research Press, 1992.

———. *The Woman in the Shaman's Body*. New York: Bantam, 2005.

Tick, Edward. *War and the Soul*. Wheaton, IL: Quest Books, 2005.

Twain, Mark. *The Autobiography of Mark Twain*. Ed. Charles Neider. New York: Perennial Classics, 1990.

Ullman, Montague, and Nan Zimmerman. *Working with Dreams*. New York: Delacorte, 1979.

Van de Castle, Robert L. *Our Dreaming Mind*. New York: Ballantine, 1994.

Von Franz, Marie-Louise. *Projection and Re-collection in Jungian Psychology*. Translated by William H. Kennedy. LaSalle, IL: Open Court, 1990.

Waggoner, Robert. *Lucid Dreaming: Gateway to the Inner Self*. Needham, MA: Moment Point, 2009.

Whyte, David. *Crossing the Unknown Sea: Work as a Pilgrimage of Identity*. New York: Riverhead Books, 2001.

Yeats, W. B. *Autobiography*. New York: Collier Books, 1965.

———. *Collected Poems*. London: Macmillan, 1958.

———. *Mythologies*. New York: Macmillan, 1959.

———. *The Trembling of the Veil*. London: T. Werner Laurie, 1922.

RESOURCES

Active Dreaming Workshops and Trainings

I lead seminars and playshops all over the world, including a popular five-day course, Writing as a State of Conscious Dreaming. I also offer a three-year training for teachers of Active Dreaming. For details, see the events calendar at my website, www.mossdreams.com.

Online Courses

I lead online courses in dreamwork and conscious living at the Spirituality & Health website, and the interactive forums there bring together a global community of active dreamers. Details at www.spiritualityhealth .com/spirit/.

Blogs

I write two blogs, post frequently, and encourage lively discussion:

Dream Gates blog: http://blog.beliefnet.com/dreamgates/
The Robert Moss Blog: http://mossdreams.blogspot.com/

Radio Show

I host the *Way of the Dreamer* radio show at www.healthylife.net.

DVD Series on Active Dreaming

The Way of the Dreamer with Robert Moss, a three-DVD set (Psyche Productions, 2005). Available from:

Psyche Productions
23 Crown Street
Milford, CT 06460
203-877-9315
www.psycheproductions.net.

Drumming CD

Wings for the Journey: Shamanic Drumming for Dream Travelers, by Robert Moss (Psyche Productions, 2004). Available from:

Psyche Productions
www.psycheproductions.net.

Audio Series on Active Dreaming

Dream Gates: A Journey into Active Dreaming, by Robert Moss (Sounds True, 1997). Also available on CD.

Please note: This audio series is an independent production with content different from that of the book (which was written afterward).

INDEX

ABOUT THE AUTHOR

Robert Moss is the creator of Active Dreaming, an original method of dreamwork, shamanic lucid dreaming, and conscious living. Born in Australia, he survived three near-death experiences in childhood and first learned the ways of a dreaming people through his friendship with Aborigines. He leads popular seminars all over the world, including a three-year training for teachers of Active Dreaming and a lively online dream school. A former lecturer in ancient history at the Australian National University, he is a best-selling novelist, journalist, and independent scholar. His seven previous books on dreaming, shamanism, and imagination include *Conscious Dreaming, Dreamways of the Iroquois, The Three "Only" Things, The Secret History of Dreaming,* and *Dreamgates: Exploring the Worlds of Soul, Imagination, and Life Beyond Death.* He lives in upstate New York. His website is www.mossdreams.com.